Featured in Cover Photo:
Cheeseburgers 30
Porcupine Meat Balls 56
Pineapple Upside-Down Ham Loaf 38

Illustrations by Karen Rolnick

The Ground Meat Cookbook

Culinary Arts Institute®
A DIVISION OF DELAIR PUBLISHING COMPANY, INC.

ISBN: 0-8326-0630-8

Contents

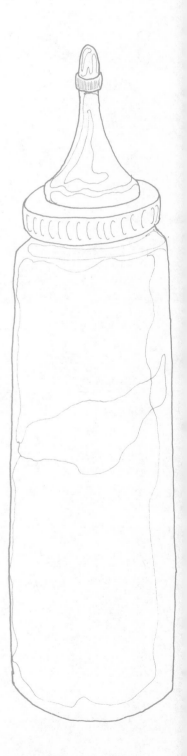

Ground Meat Cookery

QUIZ AN AMERICAN on his food preferences and you will uncover a devotee of hamburger, a lover of succulent ground meat oozing in a bun. This book is a bow to a national mania and a reminder, too, that juicy, tender, flavorful ground meats of all kinds merit top place on the menu.

For ground meats are more than hamburger, and even hamburgers can be something more than the popularly tagged "hamburger with" or "without." With imaginative combinations of herbs and sauces, for instance, they can be transformed into piquant main dishes, welcome to the plate of the most discriminating gourmet.

Ground meats have a versatility all their own. They are adaptable to the skillet, the casserole, the oven, the open fire. They can be combined deliciously with pastry, with cereal, with fruits and vegetables; piled into molds or grilled on a plank or a skewer; shaped into loaves or balls or patties; add nutrition and flavor to soup. They can start the day, gratify the lunch-time cravings, stimulate the dinner appetite or satisfy it altogether. And for busy people, ground meats have the added extra grace of cooking quickly, of supplying top excellence in a matter of minutes.

Ground meats *deserve* a cookbook of their own. And ground meat cookery, you will discover, is easy, sure-fire—and fun!

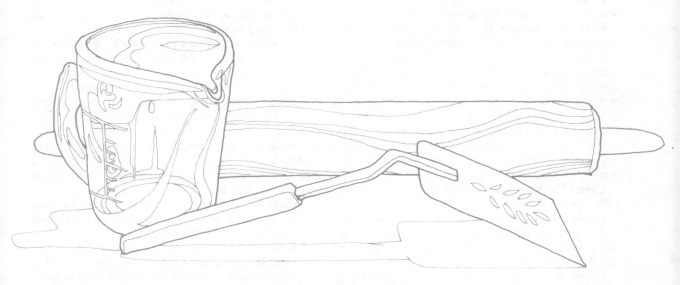

It's Smart To Be Careful

There's No Substitute For Accuracy

Read recipe carefully.

Assemble all ingredients and utensils.

Select pans of proper kind and size. Measure inside, from rim to rim.

Use standard measuring cups and spoons. Use measuring cups with subdivisions marked on sides for liquids. Use graduated nested measuring cups for dry or solid ingredients.

Check liquid measurements at eye level.

Level dry or solid measurements with straight-edged knife or spatula.

Sift (before measuring) regular all-purpose flour, or not, in accord with the miller's directions on the package. When using the instant type all-purpose flour, follow package directions and recipes. Level flour in cup with straight-edged knife or spatula. Spoon, without sifting, whole-grain types of flour into measuring cup.

Preheat oven at required temperature.

Beat whole eggs until thick and piled softly when recipe calls for well-beaten eggs.

For These Recipes-What To Use

Baking Powder—double-action type.

Bread Crumbs—two slices fresh bread equal about 1 cup soft crumbs or cubes. One slice dry or toasted bread equal about ½ cup dry cubes or ¼ cup fine, dry crumbs.

Buttered Crumbs—soft or dry bread or cracker crumbs tossed in melted butter or margarine. Use 1 to 2 tablespoons butter or margarine for 1 cup soft crumbs and 2 to 4 tablespoons butter or margarine for 1 cup dry crumbs.

Cream—light, table or coffee cream containing 18% to 20% butterfat.

Heavy or Whipping Cream—containing not less than 30% butterfat.

Flour—regular all-purpose flour. When substituting for cake flour, use 1 cup minus 2 tablespoons all-purpose flour for 1 cup cake flour.

Grated Peel—whole citrus fruit peel finely grated through colored part only.

Herbs and Spices—ground unless recipe specifies otherwise.

Oil—salad, cooking. Use olive oil only when recipe states.

Rotary Beater—hand-operated (Dover type) beater or electric mixer.

Shortening—a hydrogenated vegetable shortening, all-purpose shortening, butter or margarine. Use lard or oil when specified.

Stuffed Olives—pimiento stuffed olives.

Sugar—granulated (beet or cane).

Vinegar—cider vinegar.

How To Do It

Baste—spoon liquid (or use baster) over cooking food to add moisture and flavor.

Bath, Hot Water—set a baking pan on oven rack and place the filled baking dish in pan. Surround with very hot water to at least 1-inch depth.

Boil—cook in liquid in which bubbles rise continually and break on the surface. Boiling temperature of water at sea level is 212°F.

Clean Celery—trim roots and cut off leaves. Leaves may be used for added flavor in soups and stuffings; inner leaves may be left on stalk when serving as relish. Separate stalks, remove blemishes and wash. Then proceed as directed in recipe.

Clean Garlic—separate into cloves and remove outer (thin, papery) skin.

Clean Green Pepper—rinse and slice away from pod and stem; trim off any white membrane; rinse away seeds; cut into strips, dice or prepare as directed in recipe.

Clean and Slice Mushrooms—wipe with a clean, damp cloth and cut off tips of stems; slice lengthwise through stems and caps.

Clean Onions (dry)—cut off root end and a thin slice from stem end; peel and rinse. Prepare as directed in recipe.

Dice—cut into small cubes.

Flute Edge of Pastry—press index finger on edge of pastry, then pinch pastry with thumb and index finger of other hand. Lift fingers and repeat procedure to flute around entire edge.

Fold—use flexible spatula and slip it down side of bowl to bottom. Turn bowl quarter turn. Lift spatula through mixture along side of bowl with blade parellel to surface. Turn spatula over to fold lifted mixture across material on surface. Cut down and under; turn bowl and repeat process until material seems blended. With every fourth stroke, bring spatula up through center.

Grind Cooked Meat—trim meat from bone. Remove any excess fat. Put meat through medium blade of food chopper.

Measure Brown Sugar—pack firmly into measuring cup so that sugar will hold shape of cup when turned out.

Measure Granulated Brown Sugar—see substitution table on package before pouring into measuring cup.

Mince—cut or chop into small, fine pieces.

Prepare Bulk Pork Sausage—cut casing, if present, and remove sausage. Crumble it into small pieces with a fork when added to skillet.

Prepare Quick Broth—dissolve in 1 cup hot water, 1 chicken bouillon cube for chicken broth or 1 beef bouillon cube or ½ teaspoon concentrated meat extract for meat broth.

Scald Milk—heat in top of double boiler over simmering water or in a heavy saucepan over direct heat just until a thin film appears.

Sieve—force through coarse sieve or food mill.

Simmer—cook in a liquid just below boiling point; bubbles form slowly and break below surface.

Thicken Gelatin By Chilling—set dissolved gelatin mixture in refrigerator or in pan of ice and water until it is slightly thicker than consistency of thick, unbeaten egg white or until gelatin begins to gel (gets slightly thicker). (If gelatin mixture is placed over ice and water, stir frequently; if placed in refrigerator, stir occasionally.)

Unmold Gelatin—run tip of knife around top edge of mold to loosen. If necessary, dip mold into hot water for a few seconds. Invert onto chilled serving plate.

Unmold Meat Loaves—with spatula loosen meat gently from sides of pan. Pour off excess juices; invert onto platter and remove pan. Or, for meat loaves with topping, pour off excess juices and lift onto platter with two wide spatulas.

Whip Cream—beat thoroughly chilled whipping cream in a chilled bowl with a chilled rotary beater; beat until cream stands in peaks when beater is slowly lifted upright.

Oven Temperatures

Very slow	250°F to 275°F
Slow	300°F to 325°F
Moderate	350°F to 375°F
Hot	400°F to 425°F
Very Hot	450°F to 475°F
Extremely Hot	500°F to 525°F

Use a portable oven thermometer to double check oven temperature.

When You Deep Fry

About 20 min. before ready to deep fry, fill a deep saucepan one-half to two-thirds full with hydrogenated vegetable shortening, all-purpose shortening, lard or cooking oil for deep frying. Heat fat slowly to temperature given in the recipe. A deep-frying thermometer is an accurate guide for deep-frying temperatures.

If thermometer is not available, the following bread

cube method may be used as a guide. A 1-in. cube of bread browns in about 60 seconds at 350°F to 375°F.

When using an automatic deep fryer, follow manufacturer's directions for amount of fat and timing.

How To Cook Vegetables

Wash fresh vegetables, but do not soak them in water for any length of time. If they are wilted, put them in icy-cold water for only a few minutes. For vegetables such as cauliflower, broccoli, artichokes, and Brussels sprouts, salt may be added to the water.

Baking—Bake such vegetables as potatoes, tomatoes and squash without removing skins. Pare vegetables for oven dishes, following directions given with recipes.

Boiling—Have water boiling rapidly before adding vegetables. Add salt at beginning of cooking period (¼ teaspoon per cup of water). After adding vegetables, again bring water to boiling as quickly as possible. If more water is needed, add boiling water. Boil at a moderate rate and cook vegetables until just tender.

In general, cook vegetables in a covered pan, in the smallest amount of water possible and in the shortest possible time. Exceptions for amounts of water or for covering are:

Asparagus—arranged in tied bundles with stalks standing in bottom of a double boiler containing water to cover lower half of spears—cover with inverted double boiler top.

Broccoli—trimmed of leaves and bottoms of stalks. If stalks are over 1 in. in diameter, make lengthwise gashes through them almost to flowerets. Cook quickly in a covered skillet or saucepan in 1 in. of boiling, salted water 10 to 15 min., or just until tender.

Cabbage (mature)—cooked, loosely covered, in just enough water to cover. Cabbage (young) cooked, tightly covered, in a minimum amount of water (do not overcook).

To restore color to red cabbage, add small amount of vinegar at end of cooking time.

Cauliflower (whole head)—cooked, uncovered, in a 1 in. depth of boiling, salted water for 5 min., then covered, 15 to 20 min.

Mature Root Vegetables (potatoes, rutabagas, parsnips)—cooked, covered, in just enough boiling, salted water to cover vegetables.

Spinach—cooked, covered, with only the water which clings to leaves after final washing.

Broiling—Follow directions with specific recipes.

Frying and Deep Frying—Follow directions with specific recipes.

Panning—Finely shred or slice vegetables. Cook slowly until just tender in a small amount of fat, in a covered heavy pan. Occasionally move with spoon to prevent sticking and burning.

Steaming—Cooking in a pressure saucepan is a form of steaming. Follow directions given with saucepan because overcooking may occur in a matter of seconds.

Note: Some saucepans having tight-fitting covers may lend themselves to steaming vegetables in as little as 1 teaspoon water, no water or a small amount of butter, margarine or shortening.

Canned Vegetables—Reduce liquid from can to one-half of the original amount by boiling rapidly. Add the vegetables to reduced liquid and heat them thoroughly and quickly.

Home-Canned Vegetables—Boil 10 min. (not required for tomatoes and sauerkraut).

Dried (dehydrated) Vegetables—Soak and cook as directed in specific recipes.

Frozen Vegetables—Do not thaw before cooking (thaw corn on cob and partially thaw spinach). Break frozen block apart with fork during cooking. Use as little boiling salted water as possible for cooking. Follow directions on package.

A Check-List For
Successful Ground Meat Cookery

✔ **Purchase Ground Beef** that has been freshly ground, either regular (contains not more than (25% fat) or lean (contains not more than 12% fat). Or buy a cut of beef such as chuck, round, flank, plate, brisket, shank or neck meat and have it ground. If the cut is quite lean, have 2 oz. of suet per lb. of beef ground with the cut. A coarse single grind helps to insure extra-juicy patties.

✔ **Purchase Pork** that has been freshly ground or have pork shoulder meat ground.

✔ **Purchase Lamb** that has been freshly ground or have lamb shoulder meat or boneless stew meat ground.

✔ **Store Ground Meat** uncovered or lightly covered in the meat-keeping compartment of the refrigerator. Use within two days of purchase.

✔ **Store Frozen Ground Meat** in the freezing compartment of the refrigerator or in a freezer, wrapped in freezer wrapping material.

✔ **Break Ground Meat Block** apart with a fork when meat is added to skillet. Brown over medium heat. For small pieces, move and turn with a fork at beginning of browning process. For larger pieces, brown slightly before moving and turning meat.

✔ **Shape Balls,** burgers and loaves with a light touch. (Excessive handling results in a compact and less juicy product.)

✔ **Always Cook Pork** until well done; lean should be greyish white in color with no tinge of pink.

✔ **For Oven Products,** place oven rack so top of product will be almost at center of oven. Stagger pans so no pan is directly over another and they do not touch each other or walls of oven. Place single pan so that center of product is as near center of oven as possible.

✔ **Remove Biscuits,** shortcakes, pinwheels and rolls from pans as they come from oven unless otherwise directed. Set on cooling racks.

✔ **For Easier Slicing,** let meat loaves stand 5 to 10 min. after removing from oven.

Aids to Ground Meat Cookery

Hard-Cooked Eggs

4   eggs

1. Put eggs into a large saucepan and cover completely with cold or warm water.
2. Cover tightly. Bring water rapidly just to boiling. Turn off heat. If necessary to prevent further boiling, remove saucepan from source of heat. Let eggs stand covered 20 to 22 min.
3. Plunge eggs promptly into running cold water. Roll egg between hands to loosen shell. When cooled, peel eggs, starting at large ends.

4 Hard-Cooked Eggs

Note: Eggs are a protein food and therefore should never be boiled.

Panbroiled Bacon

Bacon slices

1. Cooking at one time only as many slices as will lie flat in skillet, place in a large cold skillet.
2. Cook slowly, over low heat, turning bacon frequently. Pour off fat as it collects. When bacon is evenly crisped and browned, remove from skillet and drain on absorbent paper. Keep hot.

Fluffy Whipped Potatoes

6	medium-size (about 2 lbs.) potatoes, cut in halves
3	tablespoons butter or margarine
½	cup hot milk or cream (adding gradually)
1	teaspoon salt
⅛	teaspoon white pepper

1. Wash, pare and cook potatoes covered in boiling salted water to cover.
2. Cook about 20 min., or until potatoes are tender when pierced with a fork. Drain.
3. To dry potatoes, shake pan over low heat. To heat potato masher, food mill or ricer and a mixing bowl, scald them with boiling water.
4. Mash or rice potatoes thoroughly. Whip in until potatoes are fluffy butter or margarine, hot milk or cream, and a mixture of salt and pepper.
5. Whip potatoes until light and fluffy.
6. If necessary, keep potatoes hot over hot water and cover with folded towel until ready to serve.

About 4 cups whipped potatoes

Whipped Potatoe Ring: Follow recipe for Fluffy Whipped Potatoes. Spoon whipped potatoes onto warm serving platter to form a ring. Draw tines of fork around ring for patterned effect.

Perfection Boiled Rice

2	qts. water
1	tablespoon salt
1	cup rice

1. Bring water and salt to boiling in a deep saucepan.
2. So boiling will not stop, add rice gradually to water.
3. Boil rapidly, uncovered, 15 to 20 min., or until a kernel is entirely soft when pressed between fingers.
4. Drain rice in colander or sieve and rinse with hot water to remove loose starch. Cover colander and rice with a clean towel and set over hot water until rice kernels are dry and fluffy.

About 3½ cups cooked rice

Macaroni

3	qts. water
1	tablespoon salt
2	cups (8-oz. pkg.) uncooked-macaroni (tubes broken into 1- to 2-in. pieces, shells, elbows or other small shapes)

1. Heat water and salt to boiling in a large saucepan.
2. Add macaroni gradually.
3. Boil rapidly, uncovered, 10 to 15 min., or until macaroni is tender.
4. Test tenderness by pressing a piece against side of pan with fork or spoon. Drain macaroni by turning it into a colander or large sieve; rinse with hot water to remove loose starch.

About 4 cups cooked Macaroni

Spaghetti: Follow recipe for Macaroni. Substitute for macaroni, an equal amount of **spaghetti.**

Pastry for 1-Crust Pie

1 cup sifted all-purpose flour
½ teaspoon salt
⅓ cup lard, hydrogenated vegetable shortening or all-purpose shortening
2½ tablespoons cold water

1. Set out an 8- or 9-in. pie pan.
2. Sift together flour and salt into a bowl.
3. Cut in with pastry blender or two knives ⅓ cup lard, hydrogenate vegetable shortening or all purpose shortening until pieces are size of small peas.
4. Sprinkle gradually over mixture, a teaspoon at a time, about 2½ tablespoon cold water.
5. Mix lightly with fork after each addition. Add only enough water to hold pastry together. Work quickly; do not overhandle. Shape into a ball and flatten on a lightly floured surface. (If dough is not to be used immediately, wrap in waxed paper, moisture-vaporproof paper or aluminum foil and place in refrigerator.)
6. Roll dough from center to edges to about ⅛-in. thickness and about 1 in. larger than over-all size of pan. With a knife or spatula, loosen pastry from surface wherever sticking occurs; lift pastry slightly, sprinkle flour underneath.
7. Loosen one-half of pastry from board with spatula and fold over other half. Loosen remaining part and fold in quarters. Gently lay pastry in pan and unfold, carefully fitting it to the pan so that it is not stretched.
8. Trim edge with scissors or sharp knife to overlap ½ in. Fold extra pastry under at edge and flute or press edges together with a fork. Prick bottom and sides of shell thoroughly with fork. (Omit pricking if filling is to be baked in shell.)
9. Bake at 450°F 10 to 15 min., or until crust is light golden brown. Cool on cooling rack.

One 8- or 9-in. pastry shell

Pastry for Little Pies and Tarts:
Follow recipe for Pastry for 1-Crust Pie. Roll pastry ⅛-in. thick and cut about ½ in. larger than over-all size of pans. Carefully fit rounds into pans without stretching, fold excess pastry under at edge and flute or press together with fork. Prick bottom and sides of shells with fork. (Omit pricking if filling is to be baked in shells.)
Bake at 450°F 8 to 10 min., or until light golden brown. Cool. Carefully remove from pans.

Six 6-in. pies, twelve 3½-in. tarts or eighteen 1½-in. tarts

Baking Powder Biscuits

2 cups sifted all-purpose flour
1 tablespoon baking powder
1 teaspoon salt
½ cup lard, hydrogenated vegetable shortening or all-purpose shortening
¾ cup milk

1. Sift togerther flour, baking powder and salt into a bowl.
2. Cut into dry ingredients with a pastry blender or two knives ½ cup lard, hydrogenated vegetable shortening or all-purpose shortening until mixture resembles coarse corn meal.
3. Make a well in center of mixture and add milk all at one time.
4. Stir with fork until dough follows fork.
5. Gently form dough into a ball and put on a lightly floured surface. Knead dough by folding opposite side over toward you. Using finger tips, gently push dough away. Give it a quarter turn. Repeat process rhythmically 10 to 15 times, until dough is just smooth. Always turn dough in same direction, using as little additional flour as possible.
6. For Use in Ground Meat Recipes—Roll, shape and bake dough as directed in specific recipe.
7. For Biscuits—Roll dough to ½-in. thickness, keeping thickness uniform. Cut with a floured cutter using an even pressure to keep sides of biscuits straight. Place on a baking sheet, close together for soft-sided biscuits, or 1 in. apart for crusty sides. Brush tops of biscuits with milk.
8. Bake at 450°F 10 to 15 min., or until biscuits are golden brown.

12 to 15 2-in. biscuits

Sauces

Medium White Sauce

2   **tablespoons butter or margarine**
2   **tablespoons all-purpose flour**
¼   **teaspoon salt**
    Few grains pepper
1   **cup milk**

1. Melt butter or margarine in a saucepan over low heat.
2. Blend in flour, salt and pepper.
3. Heat until mixture bubbles. Remove from heat. Add milk gradually while stirring constantly.
4. Return to heat and bring rapidly to boiling stirring constantly. Cook 1 to 2 min. longer.

Thin White Sauce: Follow recipe for Medium Sauce. Use 1 tablespoon butter or margarine and 1 tablespoon flour.

Thick White Sauce: Follow recipe for Medium Sauce. Use 3 to 4 tablespoons butter or margarine and 3 to 4 tablespoons flour.

Tomato-Beef Sauce

2	tablespoons fat
½	cup (about 1 medium-size) chopped onion
1	clove garlic, minced
½	lb. ground beef
2½	cups cooked or canned tomatoes, sieved
¾	cup (6-oz. can) tomato paste
¼	cup finely chopped parsley
1	tablespoon Worcestershire sauce
1¼	teaspoons salt
¼	teaspoon basil
⅛	teaspoon pepper
	Few grains cayenne pepper
½	cup (4-oz. can) sliced mushrooms, drained
½	cup water

1. Melt fat in a large, heavy skillet.
2. Add chopped onion and garlic, and cook over medium heat, stirring occasionally, about 3 min.
3. Add ground beef and cook over medium heat until browned, breaking into small pieces with fork or spoon.
4. Add slowly and stir in canned tomatoes, tomato paste, parsley, Worcestershire sauce and a mixture of salt, basil, and cayenne pepper.
5. Simmer uncovered, stirring occasionally, about 30 min., or until thickened.
6. Blend in mushrooms.
7. Simmer 5 to 10 min.
8. If sauce becomes too thick, blend in water.

About 3 cups sauce

Olive 'n' Tomato-Beef Sauce: Follow recipe for Tomato-Beef Sauce. Substitute ½ cup pitted and sliced **green** or **ripe olives** for mushrooms.

Beef Barbecue Sauce: Follow recipe for Tomato-Beef Sauce. Stir in ¾ cup **chili sauce**, ⅓ cup **lemon juice** and 2 or 3 drops **Tabasco** along with the tomatoes. Add 2 tablespoons **brown sugar** and 1 teaspoon **dry mustard** with seasonings.

Vegetable Sauce: Follow recipe for Tomato-Beef Sauce. Omit ground beef, parsley and mushrooms. Add ½ cup chopped **celery,** ¼ cup finely chopped **green pepper,** 2 tablespoons chopped **ripe olives** and 2 or 3 drops **Tabasco** along with tomatoes.

Quick Tomato Sauce

2	tablespoons butter or margarine
¼	cup coarsely chopped celery
¼	cup coarsely chopped green pepper
2	tablespoons finely chopped onion
1¼	cups (10½- to 11-oz. can) condensed tomato soup
⅓	cup water
2	tablespoons lemon juice
1	teaspoon Worcestershire sauce
2	tablespoons brown sugar
1	teaspoon dry mustard
½	teaspoon salt
	Few grains pepper

1. Heat butter or margarine in a small skillet.
2. Add chopped celery, green pepper and onion.
3. Cook, stirring frequently, until celery and green pepper are tender. Remove from heat and add condensed tomato soup, water, lemon juice, Worcestershire sauce, brown sugar, dry mustard, salt and pepper slowly while stirring constantly.
4. Simmer, uncovered, about 5 min., or until sauce is heated thoroughly.

About 2 cups sauce

Tomato-Cheese Sauce

2 oz. Cheddar cheese (about ½ cup, grated)
1 4-oz. can (about ½ cup, drained) mushrooms
2½ cups (two 10½- to 11-oz. cans) condensed tomato soup

1. Set out a large skillet.
2. Grate Cheddar cheese and set aside.
3. Drain and chop contents of can mushrooms
4. Put mushrooms in skillet with condensed tomato soup.
5. Simmer about 10 min., or until mixture is bubbling hot, stirring occasionally.
6. Cool sauce slightly and add the grated cheese all at one time. Stir sauce rapidly until cheese is melted and well blended.
7. Serve sauce hot.

About 3 cups sauce

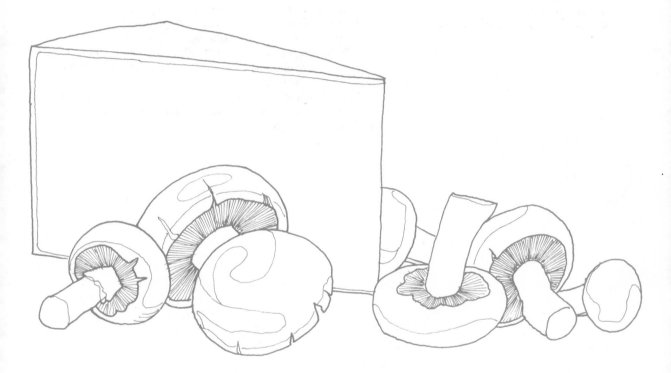

Mushroom-Cheese Sauce

1 oz. Cheddar cheese (about ¼ cup, grated)
¼ cup butter or margarine
¼ cup all-purpose flour
½ teaspoon salt
¼ teaspoon dry mustard
  Few grains cayenne pepper
2 cups milk
½ cup (4-oz. can) sliced mushrooms

1. Set out a medium-size saucepan.
2. Grate Cheddar cheese and set aside.
3. Melt butter or margarine in the saucepan over low heat.
4. Blend in flour, salt, dry mustard and cayenne pepper.
5. Heat until mixture bubbles. Remove from heat. Add milk gradually while stirring constantly.
6. Return to heat and bring rapidly to boiling, stirring constantly; cook 1 to 2 min. longer.
7. Blend in sliced mushrooms, drained.
8. Cool sauce slightly and add the grated cheese all at one time. Blend sauce rapidly until cheese is melted and well blended.
9. To keep sauce warm, cover and place over simmering water.

About 2 cups sauce

Mushroom Sauce

2	**cups Quick Meat Broth (double recipe, page 10)**
½	**lb. mushrooms**
⅓	**cup butter or margarine**
2	**tablespoons butter or margarine**
3	**tablespoons all-purpose flour**
½	**teaspoon salt**
⅛	**teaspoon pepper**
4	**egg yolks, slightly beaten**

1. Set out a large, heavy skillet.
2. Prepare Quick Meat Broth and set aside.
3. Clean and slice mushrooms.
4. Heat in the skillet ⅓ cup butter or margarine.
5. Add mushrooms and cook slowly, gently moving and turning then with a fork or spoon, until mushrooms are lightly browned and tender. Remove to a small bowl and set aside.
6. Melt in the skillet 2 tablespoons butter or margarine.
7. Blend in flour, salt and pepper.
8. Cook until mixture bubbles and is slightly browned, stirring constantly. Remove from heat and gradually add the Quick Meat Broth while stirring constantly. Return to heat and bring rapidly to boiling, stirring constantly; cook 1 to 2 min. longer. Vigorously stir about 3 tablespoons of this hot mixture into egg yolks slightly beaten.
9. Immediately blend into mixture in skillet. Cover over low heat 2 to 3 min., stirring constantly. Do not boil. Blend in mushrooms and heat thoroughly.

About 2½ cups sauce

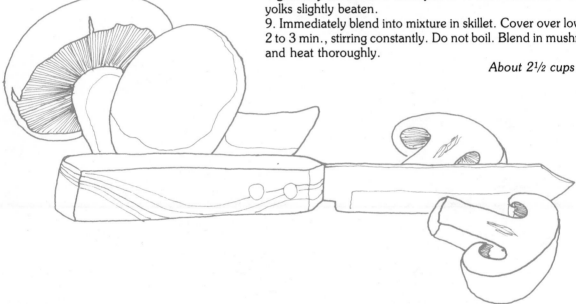

Sauce Par Excellence

½	**lb. mushrooms**
⅓	**cup fat**
1¼	**cups (10½- to 11-oz. can) condensed cream of chicken soup**
2	**tablespoons milk**
1	**teaspoon Worcestershire sauce**
1	**cup thick sour cream**

1. Clean and slice mushrooms and set aside.
2. Heat fat in skillet.
3. Add mushrooms and cook slowly, gently moving and turning with a fork or spoon, until mushrooms are lightly browned and tender.
4. Blend thoroughly condensed cream of chicken soup, milk and Worcestershire sauce.
5. Add slowly to skillet, moving mixture constantly. Simmer, moving mixture constantly, until mixture is bubbling hot.
6. Remove from heat; add sour cream in very small amounts, blending vigorously after each addition.
7. Cook over low heat, moving mixture constantly, until mixture is heated thoroughly.
8. Do not boil.

About 2½ cups sauce

Mustard Sauce

¾ cup cream or undiluted evaporated milk
¼ cup sugar
2 tablespoons dry mustard
2 teaspoons cornstarch
½ teaspoon salt
¼ cup cream or undiluted evaporated milk
1 egg yolk, slightly beaten
¼ cup vinegar
   Glazed Ham Loaf (page 38)

1. Scald cream or undiluted evaporated milk in top of double boiler over simmering water.
2. Meanwhile, sift together sugar, dry mustard, cornstarch and salt into a small saucepan.
3. Add cream or undiluted evaporated milk stirring well.
4. Gradually add the scalded milk while stirring constantly. Stirring gently and constantly, bring cornstarch mixture rapidly to boiling over direct heat and cook for 3 min.
5. Wash double boiler top to remove scum.
6. Pour mixture into double boiler top and place over simmering water. Cover and cook 10 to 12 min., stirring occasionally.
7. Remove cover and vigorously stir about 3 tablespoons of this hot mixture into egg yolk, slightly beaten.
8. Immediately blend into mixture in double boiler. Cook over simmering water 3 to 5 min. Stir slowly to keep mixture cooking evenly. Remove from heat. Add vinegar gradually and stir in.
9. Serve sauce hot with Glazed Ham Loaf. Or serve with other meat.

About 1¼ cups sauce

Apple-Sour Cream Sauce

1 cup thick sour cream
⅓ cup prepared horse-radish
1 tablespoon grated lemon peel
¾ teaspoon salt
⅛ teaspoon white pepper
1 medium-size red apple

1. Blend together sour cream, horse-radish, grated lemon peel, salt and white pepper.
2. Wash, quarter, core and chop red apple.
3. Add chopped apple to sour cream mixture and mix thoroughly.
4. Chill in refrigerator until ready to serve.

About 2 cups sauce

Horse-radish Sour Cream Sauce: Follow recipe for Apple-Sour Cream Sauce. Omit chopped apple.

Spiced Cherry Sauce

1 cup cherry preserves
2½ tablespoons lemon juice
¾ teaspoon cinnamon
¼ teaspoon ground cloves

1. Combine in a small saucepan cherry preserves, lemon juice, cinnamon and ground cloves.
2. Place over low heat and bring just to boiling, stirring occasionally.
3. Serve hot.

1 cup sauce

À la King Sauce

1	16-oz. can peas (about 1¾ cups, drained)
¼	cup butter or margarine
¼	cup all-purpose flour
½	teaspoon salt
¼	teaspoon dry mustard
⅛	teaspoon pepper
1½	cups milk
½	cup (4-oz. can) sliced mushrooms, drained
2	tablespoons chopped pimiento

1. Set out a double boiler.
2. Drain contents of can peas reserving ½ cup of liquid.
3. Set aside.
4. Melt butter or margarine in top of double boiler over low heat.
5. Blend in flour, salt, dry mustard and pepper.
6. Heat until mixture bubbles. Remove from heat. Stirring constantly, gradually add the reserved pea liquid and milk.
7. Return to heat and bring rapidly to boiling, stirring constantly. Cook 1 to 2 min. longer. Blend in the peas, mushrooms, and pimiento.
8. Cook over low heat, gently stirring occasionally, until mixture is heated thoroughly.
9. To keep sauce warm, cover and place over simmering water.

About 2½ cups sauce

Appetizers and Garnishes

Design-Your-Own Appetizers

Tempting bite-size **meat balls** may be formed out of the meat mixtures in the **Burgers and Balls** section (page 30). Cook them, insert a wooden or cocktail pick for easy handling, and serve them hot or chilled. Or arrange them in delicious combinations with other appetizers such as **Veal Picks** (page 28).

Arrange appetizers for your guests' choice by inserting the picks with balls into a holder, which can be a **grapefruit,** a small head of **red cabbage,** an **orange,** an **apple, cauliflower, eggplant** or **cheese** such as Edam. If necessary, level base by removing a thin slice from the under-side of the holder.

Garnish Meat Balls (page 27) in miniature size and savory **Big-Fellow** sandwiches (page 31) cut into narrow strips or wedge-shaped morsels are ap-

petizers supreme.

Canape Spreads (page 26) or any of the **sandwich mixtures** (page 26) spread on **buttered bread** rounds, strips, triangles or other decorative shapes cut out with cookie cutter or with a knife and a pattern make delicious appetizers. For tender, moist canapes, use fresh, soft bread; for a crunchy variety, brown the bread in **butter,** or toast and spread with **seasoned butter** before spreading with canape mixture.

Garnish attractively with **green pepper** or **pimiento, capers, anchovy fillets, stuffed olive slices, ripe olive pieces,** sieved **hard-cooked egg white** or **egg yolk,** minced **parsley** or **chives,** or red or black **caviar.**

Meat and Dill Slices

3   **large dill pickles, 5 to 6 in. long**
¾   **cup ground cooked beef**
1   **hard-cooked egg, finely chopped**
1   **tablespoon minced parsley**
1   **teaspoon Worcestershire sauce**
¼   **teaspoon salt**
    Few grains cayenne pepper
2   **tablespoons ketchup**

1. Cut ends from large dill pickles.
2. Cut crosswise into halves. Hollow out centers with apple corer and set pickles aside to drain thoroughly.
3. Grind and set aside enough cooked beef to yield ¾ cup ground cooked beef.
4. Mix lightly with beef hard-cooked egg, minced parsley, Worcerstershire sauce, salt and cayenne pepper.
5. Moisten to a heavy paste with ketchup.
6. Pack meat mixture into pickles. Place in refrigerator to chill.
7. Cut crosswise into ½-in. slices.

30 to 36 slices

Meaty Beets: Follow recipe for Meat and Dill Slices. Omit pickles. With the tip of a sharp knife or melon baller, hollow out centers of 10 tiny, drained, **pickled beets.** Add 1 teaspoon **horse-radish** with seasonings in filling mixture. Fill beets with meat mixture. Omit slicing.

Meat-Stuffed Celery Sticks: Follow recipe for Meat and Dill Slices. Omit pickles. Wash and trim 5 crisp stalks **celery.** Fill stalks with meat mixture and cut them into 2-in. crosswise pieces.

Meat Toasties: Follow recipe for Meat and Dill Slices. Omit pickles. Increase ketchup to 3 tablespoons so mixture is of spreading consistency. Set aside.
Trim crusts from 16 thin slices **bread.** Roll gently with a rolling pin to flatten. Spread bread with **seasoned butter.** Then spread each slice with meat mixture and roll. Secure with wooden picks.
Set temperature control of range at Broil. Arrange rolls on broiler rack and brush with one-half of ¼ cup melted **butter** or **margarine.** Place in broiler with tops of rolls about 3 in. from heat source; broil about 2 to 3 min., or until rolls are golden brown. Turn, brush with remaining butter or margarine and broil about 2 to 3 min. longer.

Olive-Ham Appetizer

¾   **cup ground cooked ham**
½   **cup chopped ripe olives**
1   **tablespoon thick sour cream**
1   **teaspoon prepared mustard**
1   **teaspoon Worcestershire sauce**
1   **tablespoon caraway seeds**
    Pastry for 1-Crust Pie (page 15)

1. Grind enough cooked ham to yield ¾ cup ground cooked ham.
2. Combine chopped ripe olives, sour cream, prepared mustard and Worcestershire sauce with ham.
3. Set aside.
4. Set out caraway seeds.
5. Prepare pastry.
6. Divide pastry dough into 6 equal portions; roll each protion into a 5x3-in. rectangle. Sprinkle about ½ teaspoon caraway seeds over each rectangle. Spread one-sixth of the ham mixture evenly over each rectangle to edges. Starting with long edge of each rectangle, roll up and pinch long edge to seal (do not pinch ends of roll). Place on baking sheet, sealed edge down.
7. Bake at 450°F 10 to 12 min., or until lightly browned.
8. Slice rolls; serve with radish roses and ripe olives threaded with carrot sticks.

About 30 appetizers

Ham-Stuffed Eggs

6 hard-cooked eggs
⅓ cup ground cooked ham
¾ teaspoon dry mustard
½ teaspoon salt
¼ teaspoon pepper
4 tablespoons thick sour
cream
1 tablespoon butter, melted
Paprika

1. Prepare hard-cooked eggs.
2. Cut each egg into halves lengthwise. Remove egg yolks to a bowl and mash them with a fork or press through ricer or sieve into a bowl. Set egg whites aside. Mix ground cooked ham and a mixture of dry mustard, salt and pepper with the egg yolks.
3. Stir in sour cream moistening to a thick, paste-like consistency.
4. Fill the egg whites with egg yolk mixture, leaving tops rounded and rough. Serve chilled or heated.
5. To heat, arrange egg halves, filled-sides up, in a buttered 8-in. sq. baking dish. Brush eggs lightly with melted butter.
6. Sprinkle eggs with paprika.
7. Place in 375°F oven about 5 min., or until heated thoroughly.
8. To serve, cut egg halves into smaller pieces and insert a wooden pick into each piece.

6 to 8 servings

Main Dish Deviled Ham 'n' Eggs: Follow recipe for Ham-Stuffed Eggs. Add 1 tablespoon minced **onion**, 1 tablespoon **lemon juice** and 2 or 3 drops **Tabasco** along with seasonings. Substitute 2 to 3 tablespoons **cream** for sour cream. Serve topped with **Mushroom-Cheese Sauce** (page 19).

Petite Puffs of Ham

½ cup sifted all-purpose
flour
½ teaspoon dry mustard
½ cup hot water
¼ cup butter or margarine
¼ teaspoon salt
2 tablespoons grated
Parmesan cheese
2 eggs
½ cup ground cooked ham
½ cup Thin White Sauce
(one-half recipe, page 17)
1 tablespoon capers
2 teaspoons minced onion
1 teaspoon lemon juice

1. Lightly grease a baking sheet. Set out a double boiler.
2. For Puffs—Sift together all-purpose flour, and dry mustard and set aside.
3. Bring to boiling in a heavy saucepan water, butter or margarine and salt.
4. Add dry ingredients all at one time. Beat vigorously with a wooden spoon until mixture leaves sides of pan and forms a smooth ball (about 3 min.). Remove from heat. Immediately add grated Parmesan cheese and stir until melted.
5. Quickly beat in eggs one at a time, beating until smooth after each addition.
6. Continue beating until mixture is smooth and glossy. Drop by teaspoonfuls 2 in. apart onto baking sheet.
7. Bake at 450°F 10 min. Reduce heat to 350°F and bake about 5 min. longer or until golden in color. Remove to cooling rack to cool completely.
8. For Filling—Grind cooked ham and set aside.
9. Prepare in top of double boiler Thin White Sauce .
10. Add to sauce the ground ham and capers, minced onion and lemon juice.
11. Heat mixture thoroughly in top of double boiler over simmering water. Cut top off each puff and fill with ham mixture. Replace top.
12. Serve immediately.

About 24 puffs

Liver Sandwich or Canape Spread

1   cup ground, cooked liver
     (pork, beef, lamb or veal)
1   hard-cooked egg, chopped
3   tablespoons finely chopped
     celery
2   tablespoons minced onion
1   teaspoon prepared
     mustard
½   teaspoon salt
¼   cup ketchup

1. Grind enough cooked liver to yield 1 cup.
2. Combine with liver hard-cooked egg, chopped celery, minced onion, prepared mustard and salt and mix thoroughly.
3. Moisten to spreading consistency with ketchup.
4. Spread on canape bases or use as filling for sandwiches.

About 1½ cups spread

Liver and Bacon Spread: Follow recipe for Liver Sandwich or Canape Spread. Substitute 4 slices **Panbroiled Bacon,** crumbled, for egg. Omit celery and ketchup. Moisten with 3 tablespoons **cream.**

Bologna Spread: Follow recipe for Liver Sandwich or Canape Spread. Substitute 1 cup (½ lb.) ground **bologna** (casing removed) for liver. Substitute ¼ cup **mayonnaise** for ketchup.

Ham Sandwich or Canape Spread

1   cup ground cooked ham
½   cup (about 2 oz.) salted,
     roasted peanuts, finely
     chopped
½   cup well drained, chopped
     sweet pickle
½   cup mayonnaise

1. Grind cooked ham.
2. Combine with ham, salted roasted peanuts, finely chopped and sweet pickle and mix thoroughly.
3. Moisten to spreading consistency with mayonnaise.
4. Spread on canape bases or use as filling for sandwiches.

About 1½ cups spread

Ham and Egg Spread: Follow recipe for Ham Sandwich or Canape Spread. Omit peanuts. Reduce pickle to 2 tablespoons. Mix in 2 **Hard-Cooked Eggs,** chopped, and add 1 to 2 teaspoons **prepared mustard.**

Ham-Pineapple Spread: Follow recipe for Ham Sandwich or Canape Spread. Substitute ¼ cup drained, **crushed pineapple** for chopped pickle.

Ham-Water Cress Spread: Follow recipe for Ham Sandwich or Canape Spread. Substitute ⅓ cup finely chopped **water cress** for chopped pickle and about ½ cup **cream** for mayonnaise. Add teaspoon **prepared mustard** with cream.

Petite Burgers

6	slices bread (white, whole wheat or rye)
5	teaspoons ketchup
½	lb. ground beef
1	egg yolk, beaten
1	tablespoon minced onion
½	teaspoon salt
	Few grains pepper

1. Set out a baking sheet. Set temperature control of oven at 300°F.
2. Place bread on a flat working surface.
3. Cut into 1½-in. rounds using a small cookie cutter or a knife and a waxed paper pattern. Arrange in a single layer on baking sheet and toast in oven about 15 to 20 min., or until lightly browned. Turn to brown both sides.
4. Meanwhile, measure ketchup and set aside.
5. Combine ground beef, egg yolk beaten, minced onion and a mixture of salt and pepper and mix lightly.
6. Shape into balls about ¾ in. in diameter. Place on toast rounds and flatten meat to edges of toast. Make an indentation in the center of each burger; fill with ¼ teaspoon ketchup.
7. Set temperature control of range at Broil. Set burgers on broiler rack and place in broiler with top of meat about 3 in. from heat source. Broil about 4 min., or until done.

About 20 rounds

Garnish Meat Balls

⅓	cup (about 1 rusk) rusk crumbs
¼	cup water
¼	lb. ground beef
¼	lb. ground pork
1	egg, well beaten
1	teaspoon lemon juice
2	teaspoons chopped onion
½	teaspoon salt
¼	teaspoon thyme
1	tablespoon fat
1½	qts. Quick Meat Broth (six times recipe, page 10)

1. Set out a large skillet.
2. Combine rusk crumbs and water in a small bowl and set aside.
3. Mix lightly in a large bowl ground beef, ground pork, egg well beaten, lemon juice, chopped onion and a mixture of salt and thyme.
4. Blend in rusk mixture. Shape into balls about ¾ in. in diameter.
5. Heat fat in the skillet over medium heat.
6. Add meat balls and brown on all sides, turning occasionally.
7. Meanwhile, bring to boiling Quick Meat Broth.
8. Remove meat balls from skillet to absorbent paper and drain. Add to meat broth. Cover and simmer about 20 min.
9. Serve several meat balls in each bowl of soup.

About 2 doz. meat balls

Little Sausage Balls: Follow recipe for Garnish Meat Balls. Lightly grease the skillet. Substitute ½ lb. bulk **pork sausage** (casing removed) for beef and pork. Add 1 tablespoon chopped **parsley** with the onion. During browning of meat balls, pour off fat as it collects. Serve piping hot with **French toast.**

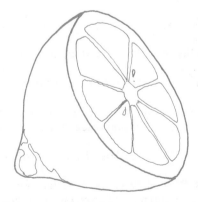

Liver Dumplings

1	qt. Quick Meat Broth (four times recipe, page 10)
1	cup fine cracker crumbs
¾	cup milk
½	lb. liver (beef, lamb, veal or calf's), sliced ¼ to ½ in. thick
1	cup hot water
1	small onion, quartered
½	cup sifted all-purpose flour
1	teaspoon chopped parsley
½	teaspoon salt
¼	teaspoon marjoram
⅛	teaspoon pepper
1	egg, well beaten

1. Set out a skillet having a tight-fitting cover.
2. Prepare Quick Meat Broth in a deep saucepan and set aside.
3. Combine cracker crumbs and milk and set aside.
4. Cut away tubes and outer membrane, if necessary from liver .
5. Put in skillet with hot water.
6. Cover skillet and simmer about 5 min. Drain. Cool liver slightly and put through medium blade of food chopper with onion.
7. Using a fork, blend liver with mixture of flour, parsley, salt, marjoram and pepper.
8. Set aside.
9. Mix cracker mixture with egg.
10. Make a well in meat mixture; add egg mixture all at one time. Mix with a fork until evenly blended.
11. Bring meat broth to boiling. Drop dumplings by rounded teaspoonfuls into broth. (Dumplings drop more readily from a moist spoon.) Drop only enough to lie uncrowded one layer deep. Cover and cook 3 to 5 min., or until dumplings rise to surface of broth. Remove dumplings with slotted spoon. Place on a baking sheet and set in a 250°F oven while cooking remaining dumplings.
12. Serve several in meat broth or any desired soup.

About 2 doz. dumplings

Burger Dumplings: Follow recipe for Liver Dumplings. Substitute 1 cup any **ground cooked meat** for liver.

Veal Picks

½	cup ground cooked veal
¼	cup pecans (about ¼ cup, ground)
1	pkg. (3 oz.) cream cheese, softened
2	tablespoons (about ½ oz.) crumbled Blue cheese
1½	teaspoons Worcestershire sauce
	Few grains paprika

1. Grind cooked veal and set aside.
2. Grind pecans and set aside.
3. Cream together cream cheese, softened and crumbled Blue cheese.
4. Combine with cheese and veal and mix Worcestershire sauce, and paprika thoroughly.
5. Shape into balls about ¾ in. in diameter. Coat with ground pecans. Insert cocktail or wooden picks and place in refrigerator to chill.

About 1 doz. appetizers

Veal-Parsley Picks: Follow recipe for Veal Picks. Omit Blue cheese. Substitute ¼ cup minced **parsley** for pecans. Roll balls in parsley before inserting picks.

Meat Puff Surprises

⅓ cup fine dry bread crumbs
1 cup ground cooked beef
⅓ cup (about 1½ oz.) grated Parmesan cheese
1 teaspoon finely chopped parsley
1 teaspoon chopped chives
2 egg yolks, well beaten
¼ teaspoon salt
2 egg whites
3 tablespoons fat
   Quick Meat Broth (page 10)

1. Set out a large, heavy skillet.
2. Prepare dry bread crumbs and set aside.
3. Grind cooked beef.
4. Combine with beef and mix grated Parmesan cheese, chopped parsley, chives, eggs and salt.
5. Beat egg whites until rounded peaks are formed.
6. Gently fold into meat mixture. Shape into balls about ¾ in. in diameter. Coat with the bread crumbs.
7. Heat fat in the skillet.
8. Add meat balls to the skillet and brown them on all sides, turning occasionally. Remove the meat balls from skillet to absorbent paper to drain thoroughly.
9. Add to Quick Meat Broth.
10. Or add to any desired hot soup just before serving.

About 1½ doz. meat puffs

Note: For best flavor, meat puffs should be cooked until very brown.

Spicy Gelatin Garnish

¼ cup cold tomato juice
1 env. unflavored gelatin
1 cup Quick Meat Broth (page 10)
½ cup chili sauce

1. Eighteen 1¼-in. muffin pan wells will be needed.
2. Pour cold tomato juice into a small cup or custard cup.
3. Sprinkle unflavored gelatin evenly over juice.
4. Let stand until softened.
5. Meanwhile, heat to boiling in a small saucepan a mixture of Quick Meat Broth and chili sauce.
6. Lightly oil the muffin pan wells and set aside to drain.
7. Remove broth mixture from heat and immediately stir in softened gelatin until gelatin is completely dissolved. Pour into muffin wells. Cool and then place in refrigerator to chill until firm. To unmold, run tip of knife around each well. Cover with baking sheet. Invert and remove muffin pan.

About 18 1½-in. rounds

Burgers and Balls

Hamburger Favorites

1½ lbs. ground beef
1½ teaspoons salt
¼   teaspoon pepper
1   tablespoon fat

1. Set out a large, heavy skillet.
2. Mix ground beef lightly with a mixture of salt and pepper.
3. Shape into 6 patties about ¾ in. thick or 8 patties about ½ in. thick.
4. Heat fat in skillet.
5. Put patties in skillet and cook over medium heat until brown on one side. Turn and brown other side. Allow 10 to 15 min. for cooking thick patties and 6 to 10 min. for cooking thin patties. Remove from skillet to warm serving platter; garnish with parsley.

4 to 6 servings

Broiler Burgers: Follow recipe for Hamburger Favorites. Arrange ¾ in. thick patties on broiler rack. Set temperature control of range at Broil. Put in broiler with top of patties about 3 in. from heat source. Broil 6 to 8 min. When patties are browned on one side, turn and broil second side about 6 to 8 min.

Cheeseburgers: Follow recipe for Hamburger Favorites or Broiler Burgers. After second sides of patties are browned, cover each patty with 1 thin slice **Cheddar cheese.** Cook 2 min. longer, or until cheese is slightly melted.

Garlic Hamburger Favorites: Follow recipe for Hamburger Favorites. Blend in 1 **egg,** beaten, and 1 clove **garlic,** slivered.

Garlic-Flavored Burgers: Follow recipe for Hamburger Favorites or Broiler Burgers. While patties are cooking, brush with **garlic-flavored French dressing.**
For Garnish—Place 6 well-drained **peach halves,** cut sides down, in skillet or on broiler rack. Brush with **garlic-flavored French dressing.** Cook 2 to 3 min. and turn. Spoon 1 teaspoon **brown sugar** into hollow in each peach half. Brush with more garlic-flavored French dressing and cook until brown sugar is melted.
Arrange burgers on warm platter. Garnish peach halves with **parsley.**

Big-Fellows

1½	lbs. ground beef
⅓	cup minced onion
⅓	cup ketchup
1	egg, beaten
1½	teaspoons prepared horse-radish
1½	teaspoons salt
	Few grains pepper
6	hamburger buns
	Butter or margarine
4	teaspoons butter or margarine

1. Mix ground beef, onion, ketchup, egg and horse-radish lightly together and a mixture of salt and pepper. Set aside.
2. Slice hamburger buns into halves.
3. Spread generously with butter or margarine.
4. Spread each bun half with about ¼ cup meat mixture. Spread mixture carefully to edges to prevent edges of bun from becoming too brown. Dot with butter or margarine.
5. Arrange the buns on broiler rack, meat-sides up. Put under broiler with top of meat about 5 in. from heat source. Broil about 6 min., or until meat is cooked.

6 to 8 servings

Big-Fellows with Cheese: Follow recipe for Big-Fellows. Spread untoasted sides of bun halves with **prepared mustard** before spreading with meat mixture. At end of broiling period, put a slice of sharp **Cheddar cheese** on each burger. Return to broiler for 2 or 3 min., or until cheese is melted slightly. Or mix ¾ cup (3 oz.) grated **Cheddar** or **Swiss cheese** with the meat mixture before broiling.

Man-Size Burgers

1½	lbs. ground beef
¼	cup minced onion
2	tablespoons ketchup
1	teaspoon dry mustard
1½	teaspoons salt
¼	teaspoon pepper
1	tablespoon fat
6	slices pineapple, drained and cut in halves

1. Set out a large, heavy skillet.
2. Combine and mix lightly beef, onion and ketchup and a mixture of mustard salt and pepper.
3. Shape into 4 large patties, about 1 in. thick.
4. Heat fat in skillet.
5. Put patties in skillet and cook over medium heat until brown on one side. Turn and brown other side. Allow 12 to 16 min. for cooking.
6. Remove burgers from skillet to warm serving platter and keep warm.
7. Place pineapple in same skillet.
8. Brown both sides over medium heat, turning occasionally.
9. Serve burgers and pineapple slices with green peas, and buttered finger sandwiches; garnish with parsley.

4 servings

Relish Burgers: Follow recipe for Man-Size Burgers. Shape meat mixture into 12 thin patties. Set out ¾ cup **sweet pickle relish.** Put about 2 tablespoons pickle relish on each of 6 patties. Top with remaining patties. Press edges together with tines of fork and cook as in Man-Size Burgers recipe. Omit pineapple.

Blue Cheese Burgers: Follow recipe for Man-Size Burgers. Shape meat mixture into 12 thin patties. Crumble 3 oz. **Blue cheese** (about ¾ cup, crumbled). Mix with 2 tablespoons **mayonnaise.** Put about 2 tablespoons cheese mixture on each of 6 patties. Top with remaining patties. Press edges together with tines of fork and cook as in Man-Size Burgers Recipe. Omit pineapple.

Drumsticks

2   lbs. ground beef
2   eggs, beaten
½   cup (about 1 medium-size) finely chopped onion
2   teaspoons prepared mustard
1   teaspoon Worcestershire sauce
2   teaspoons salt
    Few grains pepper
1   cup (about 3 slices) fine, dry bread crumbs
6   tablespoons fat

1. Set out eight 6-in. wooden skewers and a large, heavy skillet.
2. Mix ground beef, eggs, onion, mustard and Worcestershire sauce together lightly and a mixture of salt and pepper.
3. Divide meat mixture into 8 portions. Shape each portion around one of the skewers. Roll drumsticks in bread crumbs.
4. Heat fat in the skillet.
5. Place drumsticks in skillet. Cook over moderate heat, turning carefully to brown all sides. Reduce heat and continue to cook slowly about 15 min., turning occasionally.
6. Serve on warm platter or plates. Garnish with parsley.

8 servings

Triple Deck Burgers

2   cups Quick Tomato Sauce (page 18; increase water to ¾ cup)
¼   cup butter or margarine
¼   cup finely chopped onion
1   qt. (4 to 6 slices) soft, ½-in. bread cubes
3   tablespoons minced celery leaves
½   teaspoon salt
⅛   teaspoon pepper
1   egg, beaten
⅓   cup milk
     Hamburger Favorites (page 30; add ¼ teaspoon allspice with seasonings)

1. Set out a small skillet and grease a 10x6x2-in. baking dish.
2. Prepare Tomato Sauce and set aside to keep warm.
3. *For Stuffing*—Heat butter or margarine in the skillet.
4. Add onion and cook until onion is transparent, stirring gently.
5. Pour contents of skillet over bread cubes.
6. Add celery and a mixture of salt and pepper to bread cubes and mix gently with a fork . Set aside.
7. Beat egg and milk together in a small bowl.
8. Gently blend egg mixture into bread mixture. Shape stuffing into six patties. Set aside.
9. *For Meat Patties*—Prepare Hamburger Favorites.
10. Shape meat into 12 thin patties. Arrange 6 of the meat patties in bottom of baking dish; cover each with a stuffing patty. Top with remaining meat patties. Pour tomato sauce over patties.
11. Bake at 350°F 40 to 50 min. Baste patties occasionally during cooking period.

6 servings

Corn-Stuffed Burgers: Follow recipe for Triple Deck Burgers. Decrease bread cubes to 3 cups and blend in 1½ cups (12-oz. vacuum can, drained) **whole kernel corn** with stuffing.

Spicy Beef Burgers

1/3	cup ketchup
1	tablespoon prepared horse-radish
2	teaspoons Worcestershire sauce
1/2	teaspoon salt
1/8	teaspoon pepper
3	drops Tabasco
2	lbs. ground beef
2	tablespoons fat Quick Tomato Sauce (page 18)

1. Set out a large, heavy skillet.
2. Blend ketchup, horse-radish, Worcestershire sauce, salt, pepper, and Tabasco together.
3. Combine ground beef with seasonings and mix lightly.
4. Shape into 8 patties about 3/4 in. thick.
5. Heat fat in skillet.
6. Put meat patties in skillet and cook over medium heat until brown on one side. Turn and brown other side. Allow 10 to 15 min. for cooking patties. Pour off fat as it collects.
7. Serve with thin slices of onion and Quick Tomato Sauce.

6 to 8 servings

Swedish Meat Balls

1/3	cup (1 slice) fine, dry bread crumbs
1/2	cup water
1/2	cup cream
1	tablespoon butter
3	tablespoons finely chopped onion
3/4	lb. ground beef
1/4	lb. ground pork
1	teaspoon salt
3/4	teaspoon sugar
1/4	teaspoon white pepper
3	tablespoons butter

1. Set out a large, heavy skillet having a tight-fitting cover.
2. Combine, in order listed, bread crumbs, water and cream in a large bowl and set aside.
3. Heat butter in the skillet over medium heat.
4. Add onion and cook until tender.
5. Add to bread crumb mixture, the onions, butter, ground beef, and ground pork and a mixture of salt, sugar and white pepper.
6. Mix thoroughly and beat until mixture is smooth. Shape into balls about 3/4 in. in diameter.
7. Heat butter in skillet.
8. Add meat balls and brown over medium heat. Shake pan frequently to obtain an even browning and to keep balls round.
9. Reduce heat, cover skillet, and continue to cook about 10 min., shaking pan occasionally.
10. Serve meat balls hot or chilled.

About 48 small meat balls

Potluck Meat Balls

1	lb. ground beef (chuck or round)
1	egg, beaten
1/2	cup milk
1	cup fine soft bread crumbs
1	tablespoon instant minced onion
1	tablespoon minced parsley
3/4	cup finely chopped toasted walnuts
1	teaspoon chili con carne seasoning
1	teaspoon seasoned salt
1/8	teaspoon seasoned pepper
1	tablespoon cooking oil

1. Set out a large heavy skillet.
2. Combine in a large bowl ground beef, egg, milk, bread crumbs, minced onion, minced parsley, and toasted walnuts.
3. Add a blend of chili con carne seasoning, salt, and pepper.
4. Toss with a fork until thoroughly mixed. Shape mixture into 1-in. balls.
5. Heat cooking oil in the skillet.
6. Add meat balls to hot oil and brown them on all sides over medium heat, shaking skillet occasionally to keep meat balls as round as possible. When balls are cooked to desired doneness, remove them from skillet and keep warm until ready to serve.
7. To serve, dip warm balls in **Spicy Ketchup Dip** (below) and in **finely chopped toasted walnuts.**

About 3 doz. small meat balls

Spicy Ketchup Dip: Combine in a bowl and mix well **3 tablespoons brown sugar, 1/2 teaspoon dry mustard, 1/2 teaspoon ginger, 1 cup ketchup, 2 tablespoons soy sauce** and **1 tablespoon garlic-flavored wine vinegar.**

About 1 1/4 cups dip

Potato Burgers

½	lb. ground veal
½	lb. ground pork
1	whipped potato
⅓	cup (1 slice) fine, dry bread crumbs
¼	cup minced onion
¼	cup milk
1	egg, well beaten
½	teaspoon celery salt
½	teaspoon salt
⅛	teaspoon pepper
3	tablespoons fat
3	tablespoons water

1. Set out a large, heavy skillet having a cover.
2. Mix veal, pork, potato, bread crumbs, onion, milk, egg, and a mixture of celery salt, salt and pepper lightly together.
3. Shape meat mixture into patties about 2½ in. in diameter.
4. Heat fat in skillet.
5. Put patties in skillet and brown over medium heat, turning occasionally to brown on both sides. Add water.
6. Cover and cook over low heat 20 to 25 min., turning occasionally.

4 to 6 servings

Sweet Potato-Ham Burgers: Follow recipe for Potato Burgers. Substitute 1 cup whipped **sweet potato** or **yams** for white potato and 1 cup ground cook **ham** for veal. Omit celery salt. Add ½ teaspoon **dry mustard** with the seasoning mixture and ¼ cup well drained **crushed pineapple** with the meat.

Potato Balls: Follow recipe for Potato Burgers. Substitute 1 cup grated **raw potato** (about 2 medium-size) for mashed potatoes. Shape meat into balls about 1½ in. in diameter. Serve with buttered **carrots** and buttered **green beans.**

Beef 'n' Potato Balls: Follow Potato Balls recipe. Substitute 1 lb. **ground beef** for pork and veal.

Savory Lamb and Carrot Balls

3	medium-size carrots (about ¾ cup, ground)
1	lb. ground lamb
¼	cup finely chopped celery
2	tablespoons finely chopped celery leaves
1	tablespoon minced onion
1	egg, beaten
1	teaspoon salt
¼	teaspoon pepper
⅛	teaspoon sage
3	tablespoons fat

1. Set out a large, heavy skillet having a tight-fitting cover.
2. Wash, scrape or pare carrots and put through medium blade of food chopper.
3. Combine with carrots, lamb, celery, celery leaves, onion, egg and a mixture of salt, pepper, and sage, and mix lightly.
4. Shape into balls about 1½ in. in diameter.
5. Heat fat in skillet.
6. Put lamb balls in skillet and brown over medium heat, turning occasionally to brown on all sides. Cover skillet and cook over low heat about 40 min., turning balls occasionally. Add more fat if necessary.

4 to 6 servings

Lamb Burgers

1½ lbs. ground lamb
3   tablespoons minced
    parsley
1   egg, beaten
1   teaspoon salt
¼   teaspoon allspice
    Hamburger bun halves
    Onion Rings
    Horse-radish Sour Cream
    Sauce (page 21)

1. Combine lamb, parsley, egg, and a mixture of salt and allspice and mix lightly.
2. Shape into 5 patties about 1 in. thick.
3. Arrange patties on broiler rack. Set temperature control of range at Broil. Put in broiler with top of patties about 3 in. from heat source. Broil about 9 min. When browned on one side, turn and broil second side about 9 min.
4. Meanwhile, toast and butter hamburger bun halves.
5. Put broiled burgers on bun halves. Top with onion rings.
6. Arrange on platter alternately with buttered whole carrots. Garnish with parsley. Serve with chilled sour cream or horse-radish sour cream sauce.

5 servings

Bacon Ring Lamb Burgers: Follow recipe for Lamb Burgers. Set out 5 slices **bacon.**Before broiling patties, wrap 1 bacon slice around edge of each patty. Fasten ends of bacon slice with wooden pick.

Minted Lamb Burgers: Follow recipe for Lamb Burgers. Set out 2 tablespoons **mint jelly.** When lamb burgers are cooked, place about 1 teaspoonful of jelly on each patty. Broil 2 or 3 min. longer, or until jelly is melted and heated.

Lamb Buns with Tomatoes: Follow recipe for Lamb Burgers. Add ½ cup drained, sieved **tomatoes** to ground lamb with the other ingredients and mix lightly. Shape mixture into 6 patties. Split, toast, and butter 3 **hamburger buns.** Place one patty one each bun half. Bake at 350°F about 30 min., or until meat is cooked.

Ham Balls with Spiced Cherry Sauce

2   cups ground cooked ham
⅓   cup fine, dry bread crumbs
1   egg, beaten
¼   cup milk
¼   teaspoon pepper
¼   cup fat
¼   cup hot water
    Spiced Cherry Sauce (page
    21)

1. Set out a large, heavy skillet having a tight-fitting cover.
2. Grind cooked ham.
3. Combine bread crumbs, egg, milk, and pepper with ham and mix thoroughly.
4. Shape into balls about 1½ in. in diameter.
5. Heat fat in skillet.
6. Add ham balls to skillet and brown over medium heat, turning occasionally to brown on all sides. Remove from heat and add water.
7. Return to heat, cover skillet and simmer about 30 min., turning balls occasionally.
8. Meanwhile, prepare Spiced Cherry Sauce.
9. Remove ham balls from skillet to a serving plate and pour sauce over them.

About 10 ham balls

Pork 'n' Apple Balls with Noodles

1	medium-size pared apple (about ⅔ cup, grated)
1	lb. ground pork
½	cup (1 slice) soft bread crumbs
2	teaspoons minced onion
1	egg yolk, beaten
¼	teaspoon mace
¼	teaspoon nutmeg
⅛	teaspoon salt
⅛	teaspoon pepper
¼	cup all-purpose flour
2	tablespoons fat
¼	cup hot water
⅓	cup water
⅓	cup raisins or currants
1½	qts. water
1½	teaspoons salt
1½	cups (about 4 oz.) noodles
2	tablespoons butter or margarine
2	cups Quick Meat Broth (double recipe, page 10)
3	tablespoons all-purpose flour
½	teaspoon salt
⅛	teaspoon pepper

1. Set out a large, heavy skillet having a tight-fitting cover and a large saucepan.
2. *For Pork Balls*—Coarsely grated apple.
3. Combine ground pork, bread crumbs, onion, egg, and a mixture of mace, nutmeg, ⅛ teaspoon salt and ⅛ teaspoon pepper with apple and mix lightly.
4. Shape into balls about 1½ in. in diameter.
5. Coat pork balls by rolling in ¼ cup all-purpose flour.
6. Heat fat in skillet.
7. Put pork balls in skillet and brown over medium heat, turning them occasionally to brown on all sides. Remove skillet from heat and add ¼ cup hot water.
8. Return to heat, cover and simmer about 30 min., turning occasionally.
9. *For Raisins and Noodles*—Bring ⅓ cup water to boiling.
10. Add raisins or currants and again bring to boiling.
11. Pour off water and put raisins on absorbent paper. Set aside.
12. Heat 1½ qts. water and 1½ teaspoons salt to boiling in a large saucepan.
13. Add noodles gradually, stirring with a fork.
14. Boil rapidly, uncovered, 6 to 10 min., or until noodles are tender. Test tenderness by pressing a piece against side of pan with fork or spoon.
15. Drain by turning noodles into colander or large sieve; rinse with hot water to remove loose starch. Put drained noodles in a warm serving bowl. Using fork, blend through the noodles, the raisins and butter or margarine.
16. *For Gravy*—Prepare Quick Meat Broth and set aside.
17. When meat balls are cooked, remove them from skillet with slotted spoon; arrange them over noodles and set aside to keep warm.
18. Pour off fat in skillet and return 2 tablespoons of the fat to skillet. Blend in 3 tablespoons all-purpose flour, ½ teaspoon salt and 1/8 teaspoon pepper.
19. Heat until mixture bubbles. Remove from heat and gradually add the meat broth, stirring constantly. Return to heat and bring rapidly to boiling, stirring constantly. Cook 1 to 2 min. longer. Pour into a warm gravy server.
20. Serve with pork balls and noodles.

4 to 6 servings

Heart Patties with Gravy

1	egg, well beaten
⅓	cup milk
1	cup (about 1 slice) soft bread crumbs
2	cups ground cooked heart
1	medium-size onion, peeled, rinsed and quartered
2	slices bacon
1	large stalk celery, cut in pieces
1½	teaspoons salt

1. Set out a large, heavy skillet having a cover.
2. Mix egg, milk and bread crumbs together in a small bowl and set aside.
3. Grind cooked heart.
4. Put onion, bacon and celery through medium blade of food chopper.
5. Mix lightly and blend in bread mixture, heart and a mixture of salt and pepper.
6. Shape into 8 thin patties. Coat by dipping patties into flour.
7. Heat fat in skillet.
8. Put patties in skillet and brown over medium heat, turning oc-

1/8 teaspoon pepper
1/3 cup all-purpose flour
3 tablespoons fat
1 1/2 cups Quick Meat Broth (one and one-half times recipe, page 10)
3 tablespoons all-purpose flour
1/4 teaspoon salt
Few grains pepper

casionally to brown both sides. Cover and cook over low heat about 20 min., turning occasionally.

9. *For Gravy*—Prepare Quick Meat Broth and set aside.

10. When heart patties are cooked, remove to warm place and keep warm.

11. Pour fat from skillet and return 2 tablespoons of the fat to the skillet. Blend in 3 tablespoons all-purpose flour, 1/4 teaspoon salt, and pepper.

12. Cook until mixture bubbles. Remove from heat and gradually add the meat broth, stirring constantly. Return to heat and bring rapidly to boiling, stirring constantly. Cook gravy 1 to 2 min. longer.

13. Serve gravy with heart patties.

About 4 servings

Liver Balls in Onion Gravy

1/2 lb. liver (beef, lamb, pork or veal)
3/4 cup hot water
4 slices Panbroiled Bacon (page 13)
1 egg, beaten
1/4 cup milk
1/4 cup chopped onion
3 tablespoons well drained, chopped sweet pickle
1/3 cup (1 slice) fine, dry bread crumbs
1/2 teaspoon salt
1/8 teaspoon pepper
2 cups Quick Meat Broth (double recipe, page 10)
1/2 cup butter or margarine
1/4 cup chopped onion
3 tablespoons (about 1 small) chopped carrot
1 bay leaf
4 1/2 tablespoons all-purpose flour
2 tablespoons butter or margarine
1 small onion (about 1/3 lb.) peeled, washed and sliced thinly

1. Set out a large skillet and a small skillet, having tight-fitting covers.

2. Cut away tubes and outer membrane, if necessary, from liver.

3. Put liver into the small skillet with water.

4. Cover and simmer 5 min. Drain; set liver aside.

5. Meanwhile, prepare bacon in the large skillet, reserving fat.

6. While bacon is cooking, mix egg, milk, 1/4 cup chopped onion, sweet pickle, bread crumbs, and a mixture of salt and pepper, in a large bowl.

7. Crumble bacon and mix with the bread crumb mixture.

8. Grind the liver. Combine with bacon mixture and mix lightly. Shape into balls about 1 1/2 in. in diameter.

9. Return reserved bacon fat to skillet and heat. Brown liver balls in skillet over medium heat, turning occasionally to brown on all sides.

10. Meanwhile, prepare Quick Meat Broth and set aside.

11. Remove browned liver balls from skillet with slotted spoon and set aside to keep warm.

12. Melt 1/2 cup butter or margarine in skillet.

13. Add 1/4 cup chopped onion, chopped carrot, and bay leaf and cook about 5 min.

14. Blend flour into mixture in skillet.

15. Heat until mixture bubbles, stirring constantly with a spoon or fork. Remove from heat. Gradually add the meat broth while stirring constantly. Return to heat and bring rapidly to boiling, stirring constantly; cook 1 to 2 min. longer. Add meat balls and simmer about 30 min. Remove bay leaf.

16. Meanwhile, heat 2 tablespoons butter or margarine in the small skillet.

17. Add 1 small onion and cook until tender.

18. Garnish meat balls and gravy with onion slices.

About 4 servings

Loaves, Rings and Molds

Glazed Ham Loaf

1   **cup firmly packed brown sugar**
¼   **cup vinegar**
¼   **cup water**
1   **teaspoon dry mustard**
2   **cups ground cooked ham**
1   **lb. ground pork**
1   **cup (3 slices) fine, dry bread crumbs**
1   **teaspoon Worcestershire sauce**
1   **cup milk**
2   **eggs, beaten**
1   **teaspoon dry mustard**
¼   **teaspoon salt**
¼   **teaspoon pepper**
2   **whole cloves**

1. Set out a shallow baking pan.
2. *For Ham Glaze* — Mix brown sugar, vinegar, water and 1 teaspoon dry mustard thoroughly to form a smooth paste and set aside.
3. *For Ham Loaf* — Grind cooked ham.
4. Combine pork, bread crumbs, Worcestershire sauce, milk, eggs and a mixture of 1 teaspoon dry mustard, salt and pepper with ground ham and mix lightly.
5. Put meat mixture into baking pan and shape to resemble a ham. To score ham, draw knife point over meat surface forming a diamond pattern. Insert cloves in center of each diamond.
6. Pour glaze over ham loaf.
7. Bake at 350°F about 1½ hrs. Baste with glaze frequently during baking.

6 to 8 servings

Pineapple-Glazed Ham Loaf: Follow recipe for Glazed Ham Loaf. Substitute 1 cup (9-oz. can) **crushed pineapple** for vinegar and water.

Pineapple Upside-Down Ham Loaf: Follow recipe for Glazed Ham Loaf. Use a 9½x5¼x2¾-in. loaf pan instead of baking pan. Omit glaze. Spread in bottom of loaf pan a mixture of ⅔ cup firmly packed **brown sugar,** ¼ cup **vinegar** and 2 teaspoons **dry mustard.** Set out 3 **pineapple slices.** Cut two into halves. Arrange slices over sugar mixture in an attractive pattern. Pack ham mixture lightly into pan. After baking, pour off excess liquid and unmold. Serve garnished with sprigs of **parsley** and **radish** roses.

Orange Upside-Down Ham Loaf: Follow recipe for Pineapple Upside-Down Ham Loaf. Omit pineapple slices. Cut three or four ¼-in. unpeeled **orange slices** into halves. Arrange slices over sugar mixture.

Cranberry Upside-Down Ham Loaf: Follow recipe for Pineapple Upside-Down Ham Loaf. For brown sugar mixture, substitute a mixture of 1 cup whole **cranberry sauce,** ⅛ teaspoon **cloves** and ⅛ teaspoon **allspice.** Spread in loaf pan. Omit pineapple slices. Pack ham mixture lightly into pan.

Frosted Lamb Loaf

1½ lbs. ground lamb
¾ cup uncooked rolled oats
½ clove garlic, finely minced
¼ cup minced onion
2 tablespoons minced parsley
1¼ cups (10½- to 11-oz. can) condensed tomato soup
2 eggs, beaten
1½ teaspoons salt
¼ teaspoon pepper
   Fluffy Whipped Potatoes (page 14)
   Melted butter or margarine
2 tablespoons chopped chives

1. Grease a 9½x5¼x2¾-in. loaf pan.
2. Mix lamb, oats, garlic, onion, parsley, tomato soup, eggs, and a mixture of salt and pepper lightly together.
3. Pack lightly into loaf pan.
4. BAke at 350°F about 1½ hrs.
5. While loaf bakes, prepare fluffy whipped potatoes.
6. Unmold loaf onto heat-resistant platter or baking pan. Spread whipped potatoes over top and sides of loaf. Brush with butter or margarine.
7. Return to oven for 15 to 20 min., or until potatoes are lightly browned.
8. Remove loaf from oven and sprinkle chives over top.
9. For an attractive platter, serve loaf with carrots sliced with a fancy cutter for preparing lattice vegetables, cooked and glazed. Serve immediately.

6 to 8 servings

Crusty Individual Lamb Loaves: Follow recipe for Frosted Lamb Loaf. Lightly grease a shallow baking pan instead of the loaf pan. Divide unbaked mixture into 6 portions and shape each into a small loaf. Gently roll loaves in 1 cup crushed **corn flakes.** Place loaves on the baking pan and bake at 350°F about 45 min. Omit potatoes, chives and second baking.

Specialty Macaroni-Beef Loaf

1 cup (4 oz.) uncooked macaroni (1- to 2-in. pieces)
½ cup Quick Meat Broth (one-half recipe, page 10)
2 tablespoons fat
¼ cup finely chopped onion
¼ cup finely chopped green pepper
¾ lb. ground beef
¼ lb. bulk pork sausage
2 tablespoons minced pimiento
2 eggs, beaten
1½ teaspoon salt
¼ teaspoon pepper
   Tomato-Cheese Sauce (page 19)

1. Grease a 9½x5¼x2¾-in. loaf pan. Set out a small skillet.
2. Prepare uncooked macaroni.
3. Meanwhile, prepare Quick Meat Broth and set aside.
4. Heat fat in skillet over medium heat.
5. Add onion and green pepper and cook about 5 min.
6. Mix onion and green pepper lightly with broth and beef, pork sausage, pimiento, eggs, and a mixture of salt and pepper.
7. Using a fork, mix in drained macaroni. Pack lightly into loaf pan.
8. Bake at 350°F about 1 hr.
9. Meanwhile, prepare Tomato-Cheese Sauce.
10. Unmold loaf and serve with sauce.

6 to 8 servings

Veal-Oyster Loaf

½   pt. oysters
1   lb. ground veal
1¼   cups crushed corn flakes
½   cup (about 1 medium-size) minced onion
¾   cup undiluted evaporated milk
1   egg, beaten
¾   teaspoon salt
¼   teaspoon paprika
¼   teaspoon marjoram
⅛   teaspoon thyme

1. Grease a 9½x5¼x2¾-in. loaf pan.
2. Drain oysters, remove any bits of shell and chop finely.
3. Combine veal, corn flakes, onion, milk, egg, and a mixture of salt, paprika, marjoram, and thyme with oysters and mix lightly.
4. Pack lightly into loaf pan. Bake at 350°F about 1½ hrs. Unmold the loaf and serve with Swiss cheese slices. Garnish with parsley sprigs.

6 to 8 servings

Best-Ever Stuffed Meat Loaf

6   slices bread (about 4 cups cubes)
1   cup Quick Meat Broth (page 10)
1   cup chopped celery (2 large stalks)
¼   cup butter or margarine
¼   cup wheat germ
¼   cup finely chopped green pepper
¼   cup minced onion
1   egg, beaten
¼   teaspoon salt
⅛   teaspoon freshly ground pepper
1   6-oz. can (⅔ cup) tomato paste
⅓   cup firmly packed brown sugar
1   teaspoon prepared mustard
½   teaspoon Worcestershire sauce
2   lbs. ground beef
½   cup wheat germ
2   tablespoons minced onion
2   teaspoons salt
⅛   teaspoon thyme
⅛   teaspoon freshly ground pepper

1. Grease a 9½x5¼x2¾-in. loaf pan. Set out a large, heavy skillet.
2. *For Wheat Germ-Bread Stuffing*—Toast and cut bread into cubes. Set aside.
3. Prepare Quick Meat Broth and set aside.
4. Rinse, drain and finely chop enough celery stalks to yield 1 cup. Set aside.
5. Melt butter or margarine over low heat in the skillet.
6. Add the toasted bread cubes. Turn occasionally until they are coated evenly on all sides with butter and are golden brown in color. Remove skillet from heat source. To bread cubes in skillet, add one-half the meat broth (reserving remainder for meat-wheat germ mixture), the chopped celery and ¼ cup wheat germ, green pepper, ¼ cup minced onion, egg, and a mixture of ¼ teaspoon salt and ⅛ teaspoon freshly ground pepper.
7. Mix together lightly with a fork. Set aside.
8. *For Tomato Topping*—Put tomato paste into a small bowl.
9. Blend in brown sugar, mustard and Worcestershire sauce.
10. Set aside.
11. *For Meat-Wheat Germ Layers*—Put ground beef, ½ cup wheat germ, and 2 tablespoons minced onion into a large bowl. Lightly mix together.
12. Divide meat-wheat germ mixture into two equal portions. Lightly pack one portion into loaf pan. Spread Wheat Germ-Bread Stuffing evenly over top of meat layer. Lightly pack remaining meat-wheat germ mixture evenly over stuffing. Spread Tomato Topping evenly over top of loaf.
13. Bake at 350°F about 1 hr.
14. Unmold the meat loaf onto a warm serving platter. Garnish with radish roses and sprigs of parsley. Slice and serve.

8 servings

Jellied Veal Loaf

1	Hard-Cooked Egg
1¾	cups Quick Meat Broth (page 10)
½	cup (about 1 medium-size) chopped onion
½	teaspoon celery seed
4	peppercorns
1	3-oz. pkg. lemon-flavored gelatin
1	tablespoon prepared horse-radish
1	teaspoon salt
2	cups ground cooked veal
¼	cup finely chopped parsley

1. Lightly oil a 9½x5¼x2¾-in. loaf pan or a 1½-qt. ring mold with salad or cooking oil (not olive oil). Set it aside to drain.
2. Prepare egg and chill.
3. Prepare Quick Meat Broth.
4. Add onion, celery seed, and peppercorns to broth.
5. Simmer over low heat about 8 min.
6. Meanwhile, empty into a small bowl contents of pkg. lemon-flavored gelatin.
7. Strain broth and pour hot liquid over gelatin, stirring until gelatin is completely dissolved. Stir in horse-radish and salt.
8. Cool; chill gelatin mixture in refrigerator. Or chill in a pan of ice and water until gelatin is slightly thicker than consistency of thick, unbeaten egg white. (If mixture is placed over ice and water, stir frequently; if placed in refrigerator, stir occasionally.)
9. Meanwhile, grind enough cook veal to yield 2 cups and set aside.
10. Cut the hard-cooked egg into three slices and arrange in bottom of prepared pan. Spoon a small amount of the slightly thickened gelatin mixture (enough to make a thin layer covering egg slices) in bottom of pan. Chill in refrigerator until slightly set.
11. Blend into remaining gelatin mixture, the ground veal and parsley.
12. When first layer in mold is slightly set, immediately turn veal mixture onto first layer. (Both layers should be of almost same consistency to avoid separation of layers when unmolded.) Chill in refrigerator until firm.
13. Unmold as for gelatin. Garnish with parsley and notched carrot slices.

8 servings

Meat Loaf with Baked Potatoes

1	lb. finely ground beef
1½	teaspoons salt
¼	teaspoon white pepper
⅛	teaspoon Jamaica pepper
4	potatoes, mashed
1	egg
3	oz. coarsely chopped parsley
1	can (7 oz.) sliced mushrooms in water
3	oz. milk
Trimmings:	
4	medium potatoes
2	fresh cucumbers
½	lb. grated carrots
½	lb. grated white cabbage
¾	cup consommé

1. Preheat the oven to 325°F.
2. Work the ground beef with the seasonings. Add mashed potatoes, egg, parsley and mushrooms. Dilute with milk.
3. Shape into a loaf and place in an ovenproof dish and bake in the oven for about 60 minutes.
4. Add the consommé after 50 minutes.
5. Bake potatoes in the oven at the same time as the meat loaf. The potatoes will be ready when the meat loaf is. Serve with the vegetables.

Serves 4

Ham Loaf

5	**Hard-Cooked Eggs**
2	**cups ground cooked ham**
½	**can (10½- to 11-oz. can) condensed cream of mushroom soup (Pour remaining ½ can soup into a saucepan and reserve for sauce.)**
¼	**cup milk**
2	**teaspoons grated onion**
½	**teaspoon celery salt**
½	**teaspoon dry mustard**
⅛	**teaspoon marjoram**
	Few grains pepper
12	**slices whole-wheat bread**
1½	**tablespoons melted butter or margarine**
	Mushroom Sauce (page 20)
2	**tablespoon milk**
1	**tablespoon butter or margarine**
1	**teaspoon chopped chives**
¼	**teaspoon salt**
	Few grains pepper

1. Set out a baking sheet.
2. Prepare and peel hard-cooked eggs.
3. Slice three eggs and reserve for garnish.
4. *For Ham Mixture* — Coarsely chop remaining two eggs and put them into a large bowl. Grind enough cooked ham to yield 2 cups.
5. Mix thoroughly contents of mushroom soup, milk, onion and a mixture of celery salt, dry mustard, marjoram, and pepper.
6. Add to ground ham mixture and blend well. Set aside.
7. *For Loaf* — Arrange bread in several stacks on a flat working surface.
8. Trim crusts from slices. (One loaf of whole-wheat sandwich bread, unsliced, may also be used. Trim crusts and cut four equal lengthwise slices from loaf.)
9. Place three slices of bread side by side lengthwise (or one lengthwise slice of loaf) on a baking sheet and spread with one-third of ham mixture. Arrange three more bread slices on top of mixture and continue to alternate layers of ham mixture and bread until there are three layers of ham and four layers of bread. Brush top of loaf with butter or margarine.
10. Bake at 375°F about 20 min., or until thoroughly heated.
11. Meanwhile, prepare Quick Mushroom Sauce.
12. *For Quick Mushroom Sauce* — Stir into reserved soup in saucepan, milk, butter or margarine, chopped chives, salt and pepper.
13. Put saucepan over low heat and stir occasionally until mixture is thoroughly heated.
14. Using a broad spatula, remove ham loaf from baking sheet and place on a serving platter. Top with hot sauce. If sliced bread was used, pour sauce over loaf at places where bread slices join. Garnish with reserved egg slices. Slice loaf and serve.

6 servings

Ham and Veal Loaf

2	**cups ground cooked ham**
2	**cups ground cooked veal**
1	**cup cracker crumbs**
¼	**cup minced onion**
¼	**cup minced green pepper**
2	**eggs, beaten**
2	**cups milk**
½	**teaspoon salt**
⅛	**teaspoon pepper**
	Vegetable Sauce (page 18)

1. Grease a 9½x5¼x2⅔-in. loaf pan. Set out a small skillet.
2. Grind cooked ham and cooked veal.
3. Combine with ground meats and mix lightly cracker crumbs, minced onion, green pepper, eggs, milk and a mixture of salt and pepper.
4. Pack lightly into loaf pan.
5. Bake at 350°F about 1½ hrs.
6. Meanwhile, prepare Vegetable Sauce.
7. Unmold meat loaf and top with sauce. Garnish with carrot curls, pearl onions and parsley sprigs.

6 to 8 servings

Ham Ring

4	cups ground cooked ham
2	teaspoons dry mustard
1	cup milk
1	lb. ground veal
2	cups soft bread crumbs
¼	cup minced onion
3	eggs, beaten
¼	teaspoon pepper
	Horse-radish Sour Cream Sauce (page 21)

1. Grease a 1½-qt. ring mold.
2. Grind cooked ham.
3. Measure into a small bowl dry mustard.
4. Stir in to make a smooth paste, about 2 tablespoons milk from from the cup of milk.
5. Stir in the remaining milk.
6. Combine with ground ham and mix lightly, the milk mixture and ground veal, soft bread crumbs, minced onion, eggs and pepper.
7. Pack lightly into the prepared mold.
8. Bake at 350°F about 1½ hrs.
9. Unmold the ring. Garnish with pineapple slices, crab apples and parsley. If desired, accompany with Horse-radish Sour Cream Sauce.

10 to 12 servings

Ham Mousse

½	cup cold water
1	env. unflavored gelatin
2	eggs, slightly beaten
1	cup milk
1	teaspoon dry mustard
½	teaspoon salt
¼	teaspoon paprika
	Few grains cayenne pepper
2	cups ground, cooked ham
2	tablespoons lemon juice
1	tablespoon minced parsley
2	teaspoons prepared horse-radish
1	teaspoon onion juice
1	cup chilled whipping cream
	Horse-radish Sour Cream Sauce (page 21)

1. Set out a 1½-qt. fancy ring mold and a double boiler. Put a small bowl and rotary beater in the refrigerator to chill.
2. Pour cold water into a small bowl.
3. Sprinkle envelope unflavored gelatin evenly over water.
4. Let stand until softened.
5. Combine eggs, milk and a mixture of dry mustard, salt, paprika and cayenne pepper and beat together slightly in top of double boiler.
6. Place double boiler top over simmering water. Continue cooking the mixture, stirring constantly and rapidly, until mixture coats a silver spoon. (Do not overcook.)
7. Remove from simmering water at once. Stir the softened gelatin and immediately stir it into custard mixture until gelatin is completely dissolved. Cool; then chill in refrigerator. Or chill in pan of ice and water until gelatin mixture is slightly thicker than consistency of thick, unbeaten egg white. (If mixture is placed over ice and water, stir frequently; if placed in refrigerator; stir occasionally.)
8. Lightly oil the mold with salad or cooking oil (not olive oil) and set aside to drain.
9. Grind cooked ham.
10. Mix thoroughly and set aside the ham, slightly thickened gelatin mixture and a mixture of lemon juice, minced parsley, prepared horse-radish and onion juice.
11. Using the chilled bowl and rotary beater, beat chilled whipping cream until cream is of medium consistency (piles softly).
12. Gently fold whipped cream into meat mixture. Turn into mold. Put in refrigerator to chill until firm.
13. Prepare Horse-radish Sour Cream Sauce.
14. Unmold gelatin onto chilled serving plate. Garnish with pineapple slice, crab apples, and parsley.
15. Accompany the mousse with sauce.

4 to 5 servings

Corned Beef Salad

4	**Hard-Cooked Eggs**
½	**cup cold water**
1	**env. unflavored gelatin**
2	**12-oz. cans corned beef**
2	**stalks celery, including leaves**
1	**small onion**
½	**cucumber, rinsed and pared**
¼	**lemon, rinsed and seeds removed**
1¼	**cups tomato juice**
½	**cup mayonnaise**
2	**tablespoons capers**
¾	**teaspoon salt**
6	**peppercorns**

1. Lightly oil a 1½-qt. ring mold with salad or cooking oil (not olive oil) and set aside to drain. Set out a large bowl.
2. Prepare hard-cooked eggs.
3. Peel, cut into halves and chill.
4. Pour cold water into a small cup or custard cup.
5. Sprinkle env. unflavored gelatin evenly over cold water.
6. Let stand until softened. Dissolve softened gelatin completely by placing it over very hot water.
7. Meanwhile, break into pieces with a fork corned beef and set aside.
8. Cut into pieces celery, onion, cucumber and lemon and set aside.
9. Measure and put into blender container tomato juice, mayonnaise, capers, salt and peppercorns.
10. Stir dissolved gelatin and add to ingredients in blender container with lemon and onion pieces. Cover and blend until peppercorns are very finely chopped. Turn off motor (adding all ingredients at one time before motor is turned on prevents ingredients from being ground too fine). Add celery, cucumber pieces, and egg halves; cover and blend until vegetables are medium-fine. (If blender container becomes too full, empty a little of blended mixture into bowl before adding all of egg halves.) Empty contents of blender container into large bowl.
11. Turn on blender motor; add, a few pieces at a time, about one-fourth of the corned beef and coarsely chop. Empty blender-chopped corned beef into the large bowl. Repeat this until all the corned beef is chopped. Gently mix ingredients together. Turn into mold and pack gently. Chill in refrigerator 3 to 4 hours or until salad is firm.
12. Unmold as for gelatin. Garnish with ripe olives and radish roses. Place in refrigerator until ready to serve.

8 to 10 servings

Corned Beef-Cabbage Mold

2	cups ground cooked corned beef
½	small head cabbage
1	small apple
¼	cup chopped sweet pickle
½	cup cold water
1	env. unflavored gelatin
1	cup Quick Meat Broth (page 10)
2	tablespoons lemon juice
1	tablespoons Worcester- shire sauce
½	teaspoon salt
¼	teaspoon paprika
3	drops Tabasco
½	cup cold water
1	env. unflavored gelatin
¾	cup water
3	tablespoons sugar
¼	cup vinegar
1	tablespoon lemon juice
½	teaspoon salt
½	cup mayonnaise
¼	cup minced onion
½	teaspoon caraway seeds

1. Set out an 8x8x2-in. pan.
2. Grind cooked corned beef and set aside.
3. Rinse small head cabbage, finely shred and set aside.
4. Wash, quarter, core, finely dice apple and set aside.
5. Chop sweet pickle and set aside.
6. For Corned Beef Layer—Pour cold water into a small cup or custard cup.
7. Sprinkle unflavored gelatin evenly over water.
8. Let stand until softened.
9. Heat Quick Meat Broth until very hot.
10. Stir softened gelatin and add it to meat broth stirring until gelatin is completely dissolved.
11. Stir in lemon juice, Worcestershire sauce, salt, paprika and Tabasco.
12. Chill in refrigerator until gelatin mixture is slightly thicker than consistency of thick, unbeaten egg white. Stir mixture occasionally.
13. Meanwhile, lightly brush the 8-in. sq. pan with salad or cooking oil (not olive oil); set aside to drain.
14. For Cabbage Layer—Pour cold water into a small cup or custard cup.
15. Sprinkle unflavored gelatin evenly over water.
16. Let stand until softened.
17. Heat water until very hot.
18. Stir gelatin and add it to hot water stirring until gelatin is completely dissolved. Stir in sugar, vinegar, lemon juice and salt until sugar is dissolved.
19. Chill in refrigerator as directed for first layer.
20. To Complete Mold—Blend together mayonnaise and minced onion.
21. When first gelatin mixture is of desired consistency, blend in mayonnaise mixture and corned beef. Turn into prepared pan and chill. When second mixture is of desired consistency, blend in cabbage, apple, pickle and caraway seeds.
22. When meat layer is slightly set, immediately turn cabbage mixture onto first layer. (Both layers should be of almost the same consistency to avoid separation of layers when unmolded.) Put into refrigerator to chill until firm. Unmold.

8 to 10 servings

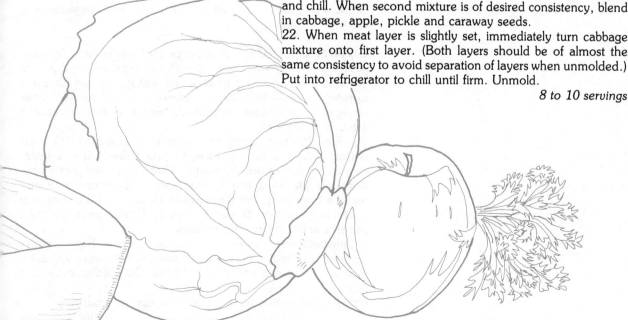

Meat Muffins

1¼ **lbs. ground beef**
½ **lb. ground pork**
2 **cups (3 slices) soft bread crumbs**
1 **cup milk**
1 **egg, beaten**
1 **teaspoon Worcestershire sauce**
2 **teaspoons salt**
½ **teaspoon thyme**
¼ **teaspoon pepper**
⅓ **cup firmly packed brown sugar**
⅓ **cup ketchup**

1. Grease twelve 2½-in. muffin pan wells.
2. Combine ground beef, ground pork, soft bread crumbs, milk, egg and Worcestershire sauce tossing lightly.
3. Add a mixture of salt, thyme and pepper.
4. Divide mixture into 12 equal portions. Pack meat mixture lightly into muffin wells.
5. Bake 350°F about 40 min.
6. Meanwhile, thoroughly mix together brown sugar and ketchup and set aside.
7. After 20 min. of baking time, spoon about 2 teaspoons ketchup mixture on top of each meat muffin and continue baking. Unmold.

12 Meat Muffins

Beef and Pork Loaf: Follow recipe for Meat Muffins. Pack meat mixture lightly into greased 9½x5¼x2¾-in. loaf pan instead of muffin pan wells. Bake about 1½ hrs. Cover top of loaf with ketchup mixture after first hour of baking period. Unmold. Surround loaf with **Brussels sprouts** and garnish with **parsley.**

Meat Ring: Follow recipe for Meat Muffins. Pack meat mixture lightly into a greased 1½-qt. ring mold instead of muffin pan wells. Bake about 1½ hrs. Omit ketchup and brown sugar. Unmold and fill center of meat ring with **potato balls** shaped with a ball-shape cutter. Garnish with **parsley.**

Petite Rings: Follow recipe for Meat Muffins. Omit ketchup and brown sugar. Grease 8 individual, ring molds. Divide meat mixture into 8 equal portions and pack lightly into molds. Bake for 30 to 35 min.
Unmold and place a spoonful of colorful cooked **vegetable** in center of each ring.

Layered Loaf: Follow recipe for Meat Muffins. Increase ground beef to 1¾ lbs., ground pork to 1 lb.; decrease thyme to ¼ teaspoon. Add ¼ cup chopped **onion,** ¼ cup chopped **parsley,** 1 tablespoon **brown sugar** and 1 tablespoon **wine vinegar** to combined ingredients before mixing. Grease a 10x5x3-in. loaf pan.
For Rice Mixture—Bring to boiling in a saucepan 1½ cups **water.** Add 1⅓ cups **packaged precooked rice,** 1 tablespoon chopped **onion,** ½ teaspoon **salt,** and a few grains **pepper.** Mix just until rice is moistened. Cover saucepan and remove from heat. Let stand about 13 min. without removing cover to allow rice to steam. Mix in 1 tablespoon chopped **parsley** and 1 slightly beaten **egg.**
Lightly pack one-third of meat mixture into pan. Top with one-half of rice mixture. Repeat layers and top with remaining meat mixture. Bake at 350°F about 1½ hrs. Omit brown sugar and ketchup.
Unmold loaf onto a serving plate. Garnish with **parsley.**

About 8 servings

Layered Meat-Potato Salad Ring

1	12-oz. can luncheon meat, ground (about 1½ cups)
3	medium-size (about 1 lb.) potatoes
2	hard-cooked eggs
½	cup cold water
1	env. unflavored gelatin
1	8-oz. can (about 1 cup) tomato sauce
2	tablespoons minced onion
2	tablespoons minced sweet pickle
2	tablespoons lemon juice
1	teaspoon prepared mustard
1	teaspoon prepared horse-radish
3	drops Tabasco
½	cup cold water
1	env. unflavored gelatin
1	tablespoon vinegar
1	teaspoon salt
¼	teaspoon paprika
⅛	teaspoon pepper
½	cup (about 2 stalks) finely chopped celery
½	cup (about ½ small) pared and diced cucumber
3	tablespoons minced onion
2	tablespoons chopped pimiento
½	cup mayonnaise

1. Set out a 1½-qt. ring mold.
2. Grind luncheon meat, and set aside.
3. Wash and cook potatoes covered in boiling salted water.
4. Cook about 30 min., or until potatoes are tender when pierced with a fork. Drain. To dry potatoes, shake pan over low heat. Peel immediately, dice and set aside.
5. Prepare hard-cooked eggs chop and set aside.
6. For Meat Layer—Pour cold water into a small cup or custard cup.
7. Sprinkle unflavored gelatin evenly over water.
8. Let stand until softened.
9. Meanwhile, lightly oil the mold with salad or cooking oil (not olive oil). Set aside to drain.
10. Heat tomato sauce in a medium-size saucepan.
11. Remove from heat and immediately stir in softened gelatin until gelatin is completely dissolved. Blend in chopped eggs, ground luncheon meat, minced onion and minced sweet pickle.
12. Blend lemon juice, prepared mustard, horse-radish and Tabasco and mix in.
13. Turn gelatin mixture into mold and place in refrigerator to chill until very thick but not completely gelled.
14. For Potato Salad Layer—Pour cold water into a small cup or custard cup.
15. Sprinkle unflavored gelatin evenly over water.
16. Let stand until gelatin is softened. Dissolve completely by placing over very hot water. Stir the dissolved gelatin and blend it into a mixture of vinegar, salt, paprika and pepper.
17. Gently mix together the diced potato and chopped celery, diced cucumber, minced onion, chopped pimiento and mayonnaise.
18. Blend in gelatin mixture. When meat layer in mold is slightly set, immediately turn potato salad mixture onto first layer in mold. (Both layers should be of almost same consistency to avoid separation of layers when unmolded.) Put into refrigerator and chill until firm.
19. Unmold gelatin. Garnish with salad greens.

8 to 10 servings

Ham Mousse

1	tablespoon gelatin
¼	cup cold water
1½	cups chicken stock
3	cups ham, chopped
¼	cup celery, chopped
1	tablespoon onion, grated
½	cup mayonnaise
¼	cup sweet-sour pickles, chopped
3	tablespoons dill
½	teaspoon white pepper

1. Place gelatin in ¼ cup water. Add chicken stock and bring to a boil.
2. Chill mixture. When it is almost set add rest of ingredients.
3. Moisten a mold with cold water and add mixture. Chill until firm.

Serves 10

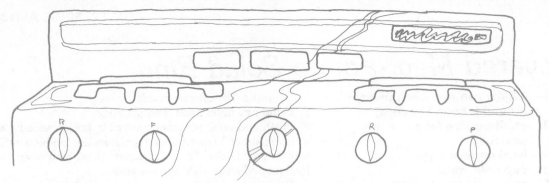

Top o' Range Cookery

Meat 'n' Cheese Blintzes

1	cup (½ lb.) ground cooked beef
¾	cup (4 oz.) cottage cheese, drained
¼	cup finely chopped celery
1	tablespoon sugar
1	teaspoon grated lemon peel
½	teaspoon salt
2	tablespoons butter or margarine
1	cup sifted all-purpose flour
2	tablespoons sugar
½	teaspoon salt
3	eggs
1	cup milk
1	tablespoon butter or margarine

1. Set out heavy 6 and 10-in. skillets.
2. For Filling—Combine ground cooked beef, cottage cheese, chopped celery, sugar, lemon peel and ½ teaspoon salt.
3. For Pancakes—Melt 2 tablespoons butter or margarine and set aside to cool.
4. Sift together flour, 2 tablespoons sugar and ½ teaspoon salt into a bowl and set aside.
5. Beat eggs until thick and piled softly.
6. Beat in the melted butter and milk.
7. Combine egg mixture with dry ingredients. Beat with rotary beater until smooth and well blended. Set aside.
8. Heat the small skillet; it is hot enough when drops of water sprinkled on surface dance in small beads. Grease skillet very lightly. Pour in only enough batter from pitcher or large spoon to thinly cover bottom of skillet; immediately tilt skillet back and forth to spread batter evenly. Cook pancake over medium heat until lightly browned on one side. With spatula, remove pancake to a plate, brown-side up. Stack pancakes. (It should not be necessary to grease skillet for each pancake.)
9. For Blintzes—Spoon about 2 tablespoons meat mixture in the center of one pancake. Fold two opposite sides of pancake to center. Begin with one of the open sides and roll. Press edges to seal. Repeat for each pancake.
10. Heat 1 tablespoon butter or margarine in the large skillet.
11. Arrange several blintzes in skillet, sealed-sides down. Brown on all sides over medium heat, turning carefully with two spoons or tongs. Remove blintzes from skillet and place on serving platter.
12. Serve hot with jam and/or thick sour cream.

About 8 servings

Spaghetti, Italian Style

3	cups Tomato-Beef Sauce (page 18)
8	oz. unbroken spaghetti Grated Parmesan or Romano cheese

1. Prepare Tomato-Beef Sauce.
2. About 20 min. before sauce is done, prepare unbroken spaghetti.
3. Place drained spaghetti into large serving bowl. Top spaghetti with Tomato-Beef Sauce and sprinkle with grated Parmesan or Romano cheese.
4. Serve with garlic-buttered French or Italian bread.

4 to 6 servings

Chili con Carne

2	tablespoons fat
½	cup chopped (about 1 medium-size) onion
1	lb. ground beef
2	cups (16-oz. can) kidney beans
2	cups (16-oz. can) tomatoes
1	tablespoon chili powder
1½	teaspoons salt
⅛	teaspoon pepper
⅛	teaspoon cayenne pepper

1. Heat fat in a large skillet having a tight-fitting cover.
2. Add chopped onion and cook 2 to 3 min.
3. Add ground beef and cook over medium heat until lightly browned, breaking into small pieces with fork or spoon.
4. Add slowly and stir in kidney beans, tomatoes, and a mixture of chili powder, salt, pepper and cayenne pepper.
5. Cover and simmer, stirring occasionally about 1 hour.

4 to 6 servings

Barley Beef Stew with Tomato Dumplings

4	medium-size carrots
2	medium-size turnips
3	medium-size onions
⅓	lb. green beans (about 1 cup pieces)
1	qt. Quick Meat Broth (4 times recipe, page 10)
2	cups water
¼	cup pearl barley
2	stalks celery with leaves, cut in quarters
1	bay leaf
¼	teaspoon thyme
2	tablespoons fat
1	lb. ground beef
1	teaspoon salt
⅛	teaspoon pepper
1½	cups sifted all-purpose flour
2	teaspoons baking powder
¾	teaspoon salt
¾	cup plus 1 tablespoon tomato juice

1. Set out a large, heavy skillet and a 6-qt. saucepan having a tight-fitting cover.
2. Wash carrots and turnips, scrape or pare and cut into lengthwise strips.
3. Peel, rinse and quarter onions.
4. Wash green beans, trim ends and cut into 1-in. pieces.
5. Set vegetables aside.
6. Bring Quick Meat Broth and water to boiling in saucepan.
7. Stir in pearl barley, celery with leaves, bay leaf and thyme.
8. Bring to boiling, cover and cook 30 min.
9. Meanwhile, heat fat in skillet.
10. Add ground beef and cook over medium heat, breaking into pieces with fork or spoon, until browned.
11. Remove bay leaf from barley mixture. Add beef and vegetables to barley mixture with a mixture of salt and pepper.
12. Bring to boiling cover and cook 20 min.
13. For Dumplings—Sift together flour, baking powder and salt into a bowl.
14. Make a well in center of dry ingredients. Pour tomato juice in all at one time.
15. Stir until dry ingredients are moistened.
16. Bring stew to boiling. Drop batter by heaping tablespoonfuls onto stew. (Batter will drop more readily from a moist spoon.) Dumplings should rest on vegetables; if dumplings settle down into the liquid, they may become soggy. Cover tightly and cook over low heat 20 min. wihout removing cover.

About 8 servings

Cheeseburgers 30; Porcupine Meat Balls 56; Pineapple Upside-Down Ham Loaf 36

Beef Balls Par Excellence

1	lb. ground beef
½	cup crushed corn flakes
¼	cup minced onion
¼	cup milk
1	teaspoon salt
¼	teaspoon pepper
⅓	cup all-purpose flour
3	tablespoons fat
	Sauce Par Excellence (page 20)

1. Set out a large, heavy skillet having tight-fitting cover.
2. Combine ground beef, crushed corn flakes, minced onion, milk and a mixture of salt and pepper.
3. Shape into balls about 1 in. in diameter. Coat by rolling meat balls in flour.
4. Heat fat in skillet.
5. Add meat balls to skillet and brown over medium heat, turning occasionally to brown on all sides. Remove meat balls to absorbent paper and set aside.
6. Prepare Sauce Par Excellence.
7. Add meat balls to sauce and heat slowly to simmering.
8. Serve on buttered noodles.

About 6 servings

All-American Chop Suey

4½	cups Perfection Boiled Rice (one and one-half times recipe, page 14)
1	cup (about 4 stalks) diced celery; cut celery crosswise into narrow pieces)
¾	cup (about 1½ medium-size) coarsely chopped onion
⅔	cup (6-oz. can, drained) sliced water chestnuts
⅓	cup slivered almonds
1	tablespoon fat
1	lb. ground pork
½	lb. ground veal
1	16-oz. can bean sprouts (about 2 cups, drained)
1	4-oz. can mushrooms (about ½ cup, drained)
3	tablespoons cornstarch
1	teaspoon salt
3	tablespoons soy sauce
3	tablespoons water
3	tablespoons molasses

1. Set out a heavy 10-in. skillet having a cover.
2. Prepare Perfection Boiled Rice and set aside.
3. Prepare diced celery, chopped onion and water chestnuts.
4. Spread out in shallow pan and heat slivered almonds in a 350°F oven until lightly toasted.
5. Heat fat in skillet.
6. Add ground pork and ground veal and cook over medium heat until lightly browned, breaking into pieces with a fork or spoon.
7. Pour off fat as it collects.
8. Meanwhile, drain, reserving 1 cup liquid, contents of can bean sprouts and can mushrooms.
9. Add reserved liquid, bean sprouts, mushrooms and vegetables to meat. Cover and cook 20 to 30 min.
10. Meanwhile, thoroughly blend together cornstarch, salt, soy sauce, water and molasses in order.
11. Pour gradually into meat mixture, stirring constantly. Bring rapidly to boiling, continuing to stir; cook 3 min. longer. Cover and cook over low heat about 15 min., moving and turning mixture occasionally with a fork or spoon. Sprinkle almonds over chop suey.
12. Serve with rice.

8 to 10 servings

All-American Chow Mein: Follow recipe for All-American Chop Suey. Substitute contents of 2 5-oz. cans crisp **fried noodles** for rice.

All-American Chop Suey with Green Pepper: Follow recipe for All-American Chop Suey. Clean 1 medium-size **green pepper;** cut into narrow strips. Add to Chop Suey when other vegetables are added. Serve over rice in large bowl.

Sausage Scallop

½ cup (about 2 stalks) chopped celery
2 tablespoons minced onion
1 lb. bulk pork sausage
3 tablespoons cold water
3 tablespoons all-purpose flour
¼ teaspoon salt
¼ teaspoon paprika
1½ cups milk
Whipped Potato Ring (page 14)

1. Set out a large, heavy skillet.
2. Prepare chopped celery and minced onion and set aside.
3. Put bulk pork sausage in cold skillet, breaking into pieces with fork or spoon.
4. Add cold water.
5. Cover and simmer 5 min. Remove cover; pour off water and fat. Add celery and onion. Cook over medium heat, moving and turning with a fork or spoon, until sausage is well-browned. Pour off fat as it collects; reserve 2 tablespoons fat. Remove sausage and vegetables from skillet and set aside.
6. Return reserved fat to skillet. Blend in flour, salt and paprika.
7. Heat until mixture bubbles. Remove from heat. Add milk gradually, while stirring constantly.
8. Return to heat and bring rapidly to boiling, stirring constantly. Cook 1 to 2 min. longer. Add sausage mixture and heat to boiling.
9. Serve in Whipped Potato Ring.
10. Or serve over baked potatoes or hot toast.

4 to 6 servings

Beef and Green Bean Caraway Stew

2 cups Quick Meat Broth (double recipe, page 10)
4 slices bacon
½ cup (about 1 medium-size) chopped onion
1½ lbs. ground beef
1½ teaspoons salt
1 teaspoon caraway seeds
1 teaspoon paprika
1 lb. (about 3 cups) green beans
½ cup liquid (cooled bean cooking liquid plus water)
¼ cup all-purpose flour
½ cup thick sour cream

1. Set out a large, heavy skillet having a tight-fitting cover.
2. Prepare Quick Meat Broth and set aside.
3. Cut bacon into ½-in. pieces.
4. Put bacon in skillet with chopped onion.
5. Place over medium heat until bacon is partially cooked, moving and turning the mixture with a spoon or fork. Add ground beef and cook over medium heat until browned, breaking into pieces with fork or spoon.
6. Remove from heat and blend in the meat broth and a mixture of salt, caraway seeds and paprika.
7. Cover skillet and simmer 30 min.
8. Meanwhile, wash green beans, remove and discard ends and cut into 1-in. pieces.
9. Cook about 15 min., or until just tender. Drain, if necessary, reserving cooking liquid and set aside. Cool cooking liquid.
10. Pour liquid (cooled bean cooking liquid plus water) into a 1-pt. screw-top jar.
11. Sprinkle flour evenly over liquid.
12. Cover tightly and shake until mixture is well blended. Bring contents of skillet to boiling. Shake flour mixture and add slowly to skillet, stirring constantly. Bring to boiling; cook 3 to 5 min. longer. Remove from heat and vigorously stir about ½ cup of the mixture, 1 tablespoon at a time, into sour cream.
13. Pour the mixture gradually into the skillet while stirring constantly. Gently mix in green beans. Cook over low heat, moving mixture gently, 3 to 5 min., until heated thoroughly.
14. Do not boil.

5 to 7 servings

Crusty Croquettes

1½ cups Thick White Sauce (1½ times recipe, page 17)
2 cups ground cooked beef, veal or lamb
2 medium-size carrots, washed and pared or scraped
2 stalks celery with leaves, cut in pieces
1 medium-size onion, quartered
½ teaspoon salt
¼ teaspoon marjoram
1 cup (about 3 slices) fine, dry bread crumbs
1 egg, slightly beaten
2 tablespoons milk or water
Hydrogenated vegetable shortening, all-purpose shortening, lard or cooking oil for deep-frying
Tomato-Cheese Sauce (page 19)

1. Prepare Thick White Sauce and set aside to cool.
2. Meanwhile, grind cooked beef, veal or lamb.
3. Put through medium blade of food chopper carrots, celery and onion.
4. Combine sauce, meat and vegetables; mix lightly together. Blend in a mixture of salt and marjoram.
5. Put in refrigerator to chill 1 hr.
6. Allowing about ⅓ cup mixture for each, shape into rolls, balls or cones. Roll in a shallow pan containing dry bread crumbs.
7. Dip into mixture of egg and milk or water.
8. Roll again in crumbs. Return to refrigerator to chill about 40 min. longer.
9. About 20 min. before deep-frying fill a deep saucepan one-half to two-thirds full with hydrogenated vegetable shortening, all purpose shortening, lard or cooking oil for deep-frying.
10. Heat slowly to 375°F.
11. Deep-fry only as many croquettes at one time as will lie flat and uncrowded, one layer deep in fat. Turn frequently to brown evenly. Deep-fry 5 to 7 min., or until golden brown; drain over fat before removing to absorbent paper.
12. Serve immediately accompanied with Tomato-Cheese Sauce.

5 servings

Oven Croquettes: Follow recipe for Crusty Croquettes. Omit deep-frying. Set coated, chilled croquettes in a shallow, greased baking pan. Brush croquettes with 3 to 4 tablespoons **butter** or **margarine,** melted. Bake at 400°F 20 to 25 min., or until golden brown.

Indian Rice and Meat Dish

Rice
1 tablespoon butter or margarine
1 cup long-grained rice
2-3 teaspoons curry
2 cups water
1 teaspoon salt

2 tablespoons butter or margarine
2 teaspoons curry
1 lb. ground beef
1 teaspoon salt
½ teaspoon black pepper, freshly ground
1 small fresh cucumber chutney
3 eggs

1. Melt the butter or margarine in a saucepan. Stir in curry, then the rice until rice is well coated with curry. Pour on cold water, add salt and bring to a rapid boil while stirring. Put cover on saucepan and let rice boil over a very low heat for 20 minutes. Remove pan from heat and fluff it with two forks.
2. Meanwhile brown butter or margarine in a large, heavy frying pan. Put the ground beef in the pan, crumble it with a wooden fork and let meat brown while stirring. Season with salt, pepper and curry.
3. Rinse and cut the cucumber into ¼″ long strips. Stir the cucumber strips into the meat mixture and stir carefully with two forks.
4. Stir in the rice and toss gently. Make 3 dents in the mixture and slip 3 eggs slowly into the dents. Let pan stand on a low heat covered until the eggs have set, about 10 minutes. Serve with **chutney** and a **fruit salad.**

Serves 4

Curried Lamb with Apple

1½	cups Perfection Boiled Rice (one-half recipe, omit drying.)
1	tablespoon fat
1	lb. ground lamb
¼	cup finely chopped celery
3	tablespoons finely chopped onion
2	cups Quick Chicken Broth (double recipe, page 10)
½	cup water
¼	cup all-purpose flour
1½	teaspoons salt
1	teaspoon curry powder
¼	teaspoon ginger
⅛	teaspoon nutmeg
	Few grains cayenne pepper
1	medium-size apple (about 1 cup, sliced)
½	cup moist flaked coconut

1. Set out a large, heavy skillet.
2. Prepare Perfection Boiled Rice.
3. Meanwhile, heat fat in the skillet.
4. Add ground lamb and cook over medium heat until lightly browned breaking into small pieces with fork or spoon.
5. Pour off fat as it collects in skillet.
6. Add to skillet chopped celery and onion.
7. Cook slowly, moving and turning mixture occasionally, until celery is tender.
8. Meanwhile, prepare Quick Chicken Broth.
9. Add to lamb mixture and simmer.
10. Put water into a 1-pt. screw-top jar.
11. Sprinkle evenly onto water a mixture of all-purpose flour, salt, curry powder, ginger, nutmeg and cayenne pepper.
12. Cover jar tightly; shake until well blended. Bring lamb mixture to boiling; shake flour mixture and pour slowly into the skillet; keep mixture moving with a fork or spoon. Bring to boiling. Cook 3 to 5 min.
13. Wash, quarter, core, pare and slice apple.
14. Add to lamb mixture. Thoroughly mix the lamb mixture and rice and turn into a warm serving bowl. Sprinkle top with moist flaked coconut.
15. Serve immediately.

6 to 8 servings

Stuffed Cabbage Rolls

8	large cabbage leaves
½	teaspoon salt
3	tablespoons butter or margarine
1	cup (about 2 medium-size) finely chopped onion
⅔	lb. ground beef (break into small pieces with fork or spoon)
⅔	cup packaged precooked rice
¾	teaspoon salt
½	teaspoon Worcestershire sauce
⅛	teaspoon pepper
3½	cups (28-oz. can) tomatoes, sieved
1	bay leaf
1	clove garlic, uncut(insert wooden pick for easy removal)
½	teaspoon salt
	Few grains pepper

1. Grease a shallow, 2-qt. top-of-range casserole having a tight-fitting cover. Set out a large saucepan having a tight-fitting cover and a medium-size skillet.
2. From a head of cabbage remove and wash leaves.
3. Pour boiling water into the large saucepan to 1-in. level. Add cabbage leaves and ½ teaspoon salt.
4. Cover and simmer 2 to 3 min., or until leaves begin to soften; drain.
5. Meanwhile, heat butter or margarine in skillet.
6. Add and cook onion until tender.
7. Remove from heat and mix beef, rice, and a mixture of salt, Worcestershire sauce and pepper thoroughly.
8. Place about ¼ cup of the mixture in center of each cabbage leaf. Roll each leaf, tucking ends in toward center. Fasten securely with wooden picks; place in casserole. Pour over cabbage rolls a mixture of tomatoes, bay leaf, garlic, salt and pepper.
9. Cover and simmer 45 to 60 min., or until rolls are tender. Place rolls in warm serving dish. Remove wooden picks, garlic and bay leaf. Spoon sauce over rolls.

4 servings

Lamb-Stuffed Cabbage Rolls: Follow recipe for Stuffed Cabbage Rolls. Substitute ⅔ lb. ground **lamb** for beef.

Oven Main Dishes

Planked Ground Meat Dinner

Fluffy Whipped Potatoes
6   **medium-size (about 1½ lbs.) onions**
2   **large (about 1 lb.) tomatoes**
1   **lb. ground beef**
¼   **cup milk or water**
2   **teaspoons Worcestershire sauce**
1   **teaspoon salt**
⅛   **teaspoon pepper**
  Melted butter or margarine
3   **slices Panbroiled Bacon (page 13)**

1. *To Season a New Plank*—Brush a hardwood plank with unsalted fat. Heat in 250°F oven for 1 hr. Cool and store until used.
2. *For Vegetables*—Prepare Fluffy Whipped Potatoes and set aside to keep warm.
3. Cut off roots and a thin slice from each stem end of onions.
4. Peel, rinse and cook 20 to 30 min., or just until tender. Drain the onions; set aside and keep warm.
5. Rinse and cut off stem ends from tomatoes.
6. Cut into halves crosswise and set aside.
7. *For Meat*—Mix beef, milk or water, Worcestershire sauce, and a mixture of salt and pepper lightly together.
8. Put meat mixture on broiler rack and pat into a large oval about 1½-in. thick, or shape to resemble a steak.
9. Grease the seasoned plank with unsalted fat. Heat in oven while broiling meat.
10. Set temperature control of range at Broil. Put meat under broiler with top of meat about 3 in. from heat source. Broil about 10 to 12 min. When meat is browned on one side, remove from broiler and place meat, browned side down, in center of the heated plank. Surround with the cooked whole onions and tomato halves. Force whipped potatoes through a pastry bag and a No. 7 star tube to form a border around meat and vegetables. Cover exposed plank as completely as possible.
11. Brush onion, tomatoes, and potatoes with butter or margarine.
12. Place plank under broiler with top of meat about 3 in. from source of heat. Broil about 8 min., or until meat is browned and potatoes are lightly browned.
13. Meanwhile, prepare Panbroiled Bacon.
14. Remove plank from oven and put on a serving tray. Arrange bacon on top.

4 servings

Acorn Squash Entree

2   **medium-size (about 1½ lbs. each) acorn squash Boiling water to ½ in. level**
1   **lb. bulk pork sausage (page 10)**
⅔   **cup (2 slices) fine, dry bread crumbs**
½   **cup undiluted evaporated milk**
1   **egg, beaten**
2   **tablespoons water**
1   **cup whole cranberry sauce**
¼   **cup firmly packed brown sugar**
1   **tablespoon vinegar**

1. Set out a skillet, having a cover, and a shallow baking dish.
2. With a sharp, heavy knife, split acorn squash into crosswise halves.
3. Cut a thin slice from bottom of each half so that halves will stand upright. Remove seed sections. Place squash, cavity-side down, in baking dish. Pour boiling water into baking dish.
4. Bake at 400°F 25 to 30 min.
5. Meanwhile, mix pork sausage, bread crumbs, milk and egg lightly and shape into 4 patties about ¾ in. thick.
6. Put patties in cold skillet; add 2 tablespoons water.
7. Cover skillet and cook slowly 5 min. Remove cover; pour off liquid. Lightly brown patties over medium heat, turning frequently to brown both sides, and pouring off fat as it collects. Remove patties to absorbent paper. Drain any remaining fat from skillet and wipe skillet with absorbent paper.
8. Blend cranberry sauce, brown sugar and vinegar together in skillet.
9. Heat slowly, stirring to blend. Bring to boiling. Cook 2 to 3 min., stirring constantly.
10. Remove squash from oven; reduce temperature to 350°F. Drain squash and turn them cavity-side up. Brush inside of squash with part of cranberry mixture. Press a sausage patty into each squash half. Spoon a small amount of remaining cranberry mixture over each patty. Return to oven and bake 25 to 30 min., or until squash is tender.
11. Serve with cranberry sauce.

4 servings

Acorn Squash with Sausage Stuffing:

Follow recipe for Acorn Squash Entree through first baking process of squash. With spoon, scoop cooked squash from shells; do not break skin. Omit bread crumbs, evaporated milk, egg and water. Brown sausage in skillet, breaking into small pieces with fork or spoon as it browns. Add to skillet ½ cup (about 1 medium-size) chopped **onion.** Cook until the onion is tender. Mix squash, 3 tablespoons undiluted **evaporated milk,** ½ teaspoon **salt** and ¼ teaspoon **thyme** with sausage-onion mixture. Pile mixture lightly into squash shells. Bake at 350°F 10 to 15 min., or until squash is lightly browned.

Savory Sausage Cutlets

1 **cup Perfection Boiled Rice (one-third recipe, page 14)**
1 **lb. bulk pork sausage (page 10)**
1 **cup Thick White Sauce (page 17)**
1 **oz. Cheddar cheese (about ¼ cup, grated)**
2 **tablespoons minced parsley**
⅔ **cup (2 slices) fine, dry bread crumbs**
1 **egg, slightly beaten**
2 **tablespoons milk or water Apple-Sour Cream Sauce (page 21) or Mustard Sauce (page 21)**

1. Set out a large, heavy skillet and an 11x7x1½-in. baking pan.
2. Prepare Perfection Boiled Rice.
3. Meanwhile, put pork sausage in cold skillet.
4. Cook over medium heat, breaking into pieces with fork or spoon. Pour off fat as it collects, reserving 4 tablespoons. When sausage is lightly browned, remove to absorbent paper and set aside.
5. Using reserved fat, prepare Thick White Sauce.
6. Cool slightly.
7. Grate Cheddar cheese.
8. Add all at one time to white sauce and stir until cheese is melted and well blended. Mix into sauce, the sausage, rice and parsley.
9. Put in refrigerator to chill for 1 to 2 hrs.
10. Divide chilled mixture into 6 portions. Put on waxed paper. To form cutlets, pat each portion into a ½-in. thick round. Coat cutlets by dipping into bread crumbs.
11. Dip cutlets into a mixture of egg and milk or water.
12. Coat again in remaining bread crumbs. Put in baking dish.
13. Bake at 350°F 25 to 30 min., or until lightly browned. If desired, serve with Apple-Sour Cream Sauce or Mustard Sauce.

6 servings

Cranberry Sausage Cutlets: Follow recipe for Savory Sausage Cutlets. Pour 2 cups (16-oz. can) whole **cranberry sauce** into bottom of baking pan. Arrange breaded cutlets over sauce and bake as in recipe.

Porcupine Beef Balls

2 **cups Quick Tomato Sauce (page 18; add ½ cup water)**
1 **lb. ground beef**
½ **cup uncooked rice**
¼ **cup minced onion**
1 **teaspoon salt**
⅛ **teaspoon pepper**

1. Lightly grease a 2½-qt. casserole having a tight-fitting cover.
2. Prepare and set aside Quick Tomato Sauce; add ½ cup water).
3. Meanwhile, combine beef, rice, onion and a mixture of salt and pepper and mix lightly.
4. Shape into 1½-in. balls and put in casserole. Pour tomato sauce over meat balls.
5. Cover and bake at 350°F about 1 hr., or until visible rice is tender when pressed lightly between fingers.
6. To serve, garnish with parsley.

4 to 6 servings

Porcupine Beef Balls with Mushrooms: Follow recipe for Porcupine Beef Balls. Substitute a mixture of 1¼ cups (10½- to 11-oz. can) **condensed cream of**

mushroom soup and 1 cup water for the Quick Tomato Sauce.

Porcupine Beef Balls with Celery: Follow recipe for Porcupine Beef Balls. Add ½ teaspoon **celery** salt with the seasonings in beef balls. Substitute a mixture of 1½ cups (10½- to 11-oz. can) **condensed cream of celery soup** and 1 cup **water** for the Quick Tomato Sauce.

Spaghetti and Meat Balls

3	tablespoons butter or margarine
½	cup (about 1 medium-size) chopped onion
1	clove garlic, minced
3½	cups (28-oz. can) tomatoes, sieved
¾	cup (6-oz. can) tomato paste
1	teaspoon salt
⅛	teaspoon pepper
⅛	teaspoon oregano
½	cup (2 oz.) grated Parmesan cheese
½	lb. ground beef
½	lb. ground pork
1	cup (1½ slices) soft bread crumbs
1	egg, beaten
2	tablespoons minced parsley
¾	teaspoon salt
⅛	teaspoon pepper
2	tablespoons all-purpose flour
3	tablespoons butter or margarine
4	oz. unbroken spaghetti (one-half recipe, page 14)

1. Grease a 2-qt. casserole. Set out a large, heavy skillet having a tight-fitting cover.
2. Heat 3 tablespoons butter or margarine in a large saucepan.
3. Add onion and garlic and cook over medium heat, stirring occasionally, until onion is tender.
4. Remove from heat and stir in tomatoes, tomato paste, and a mixture of salt, pepper and oregano.
5. Simmer 1 hr., stirring occasionally.
6. Meanwhile, set out Parmesan cheese.
7. Lightly mix one-half of grated cheese with beef, pork, bread crumbs, egg, parsley, and a mixture of salt and pepper.
8. Shape meat mixture into balls about ¾ in. in diameter. Coat by rolling in flour.
9. Heat 2 or 3 tablespoons butter or margarine in skillet.
10. Add meat balls and brown over medium heat. Shake pan frequently to secure an even browning and to keep balls round. Pour off fat as it collects. Pour sauce over meat balls, cover and cook over low heat 20 min. longer.
11. Meanwhile prepare spaghetti.
12. Place drained spaghetti in bottom of casserole. Spoon sauce and meat balls over spaghetti. Sprinkle with remaining ¼ cup grated cheese.
13. Bake at 325°F 15 to 20 min.
14. Serve with additional grated cheese.

6 to 8 servings

Meat-Stuffed Manicotti

2 tablespoons olive oil
½ pound fresh spinach, washed, dried, and finely chopped
2 tablespoons chopped onion
½ teaspoon salt
½ teaspoon oregano
½ pound ground beef
2 tablespoons fine dry bread crumbs
1 egg, slightly beaten
1 can (6 ounces) tomato paste
8 manicotti shells (two thirds of a 5½-ounce package), cooked and drained
1½ tablespoons butter, softened (optional)
1 to 2 tablespoons grated Parmesan or Romano cheese (optional)
  Mozzarella cheese, shredded

1. Heat olive oil in a skillet. Add spinach, onion salt, oregano, and meat. Mix well, separating meat into small pieces. Cook, stirring frequently, until meat is no longer pink.

2. Set aside to cool slightly. Add bread crumbs, egg, and 2 tablespoons tomato paste; mix well. Stuff manicotti with mixture. Put side by side in a greased 2-quart baking dish. If desired, spread butter over stuffed manicotti and sprinkle with the grated cheese.

3. Spoon remaining tomato paste on top of the manicotti down the center of the dish. Sprinkle mozzarella cheese on top of tomato paste. Cover baking dish.

4. Bake at 425°F. 12 to 15 minutes, or until mozzarella melts.

4 servings

Pâté à La Maison Grand Vefour

Dough
2 cups flour
1 egg
3 oz. water
7 oz. butter
  salt

Filling
1 lb. ground veal
1 lb. ground pork
2 egg yolks
  salt
  pepper
  chervil
  tarragon
  chopped parsley
½ lb. cooked ham
  chopped truffles

1. Combine all ingredients for the dough and roll out to ⅓″ thick.

2. For the filling make a mixture of the ground meat by grinding veal, and pork together, add egg yolks, and season with salt and pepper and the other spices.

3. Add the cooked ham and the truffles, and place the mixture on the dough.

4. Roll the dough around the mixture (save a little for decoration) and pinch it together at both ends. Place it on a baking sheet. Cut a small strip of the dough and make a band. Place it on top of the roll where the dough sides are overlapping. Seal the band with a beaten egg. This band will keep the dough sealed.

5. Put two "chimneys" of waxed paper in the roll. This will allow all the liquid to evaporate and the paté will be firm.

6. Bake in a medium hot oven (350°-400°F.) for about 1½ hours, for a paté of 4 lbs.

7. Remove the "chimneys". Cover the holes with small decorative lids made from leftover dough and brown.

Serves 6

Green Peppers with Ham-Rice Stuffing

4	large green peppers
2	cups ground cooked ham
1	cup Perfection Boiled Rice (one-third recipe, page 14)
¼	lb. Cheddar cheese
½	cup butter or margarine
2	tablespoons minced onion
¼	teaspoon dry mustard
¼	teaspoon garlic salt
1½	cups tomato juice

1. Set out a shallow 2-qt. baking dish and a medium-size saucepan.
2. Rinse peppers and cut into halves lengthwise.
3. With a knife remove stem, white fiber and seeds. Rinse cavities. Drop pepper halves into boiling salted watter to cover and simmer 5 min. Remove peppers from water and invert. Set aside to drain.
4. While peppers are cooking, grind ham and set aside.
5. Prepare Perfection Boiled Rice.
6. Meanwhile, cut Cheddar cheese into 8 slices and set aside.
7. Melt butter or margarine in the saucepan.
8. Add ham and toss lightly with a fork to blend.
9. Blend in rice and onion.
10. Mix and blend in dry mustard and garlic salt.
11. Lightly fill peppers with ham-rice mixture, heaping slightly. Place one slice of cheese on top of each pepper. Place pappers in the baking dish. Pour tomato juice around peppers.
12. Bake at 350°F about 20 min. Increase heat to 400°F and bake 10 min. longer, or until cheese is lightly browned.
13. If desired, spoon the hot tomato juice over stuffed peppers.

4 servings

Ham-Corn Stuffed Peppers: Follow recipe for Green Peppers with Ham-Rice Stuffing. Omit butter, rice and seasonings. Mix lightly with the ham and onion, 1½ cups (contents of 12-oz. vacuum can, drained) **whole kernel corn,** ½ cup (about ½ slice) soft **bread crumbs,** ¼ teaspoon **salt** and few grains **pepper.** Gently mix in with a fork 2 well-beaten **eggs.** Omit cheese. Cut 4 slices **bacon** into halves and place one-half slice on top of each filled pepper. **Water** may be substituted for tomato juice.

Lamb Soufflé

2	cups ground cooked lamb
1	cup Thick White Sauce (page 17); add ½ teaspoon onion salt and ⅛ teaspoon nutmeg with seasonings
4	egg yolks
3	tablespoons minced parsley
4	egg whites

1. Set out a 1½-qt. casserole; do not grease. Heat water for hot water bath.
2. Grind cooked lamb.
3. Prepare Thick White Sauce.
4. Blend ground lamb into white sauce.
5. Beat egg until very thick and lemon colored.
6. Slowly spoon sauce into beaten egg yolks, while beating vigorously with a spoon. Mix or blend in 3 tablespoons minced parsley.
7. Beat egg whites until rounded peaks are formed and egg whites do not slide when bowl is partially inverted.
8. Gently spread sauce over beaten egg whites. Carefully fold together until just blended. Turn mixture into casserole. Put casserole in the hot water bath.
9. Bake at 350°F 40 to 50 min., or until a silver knife comes out clean when inserted half between center and edge of casserole.
10. Serve at once.

6 to 8 servings

Flavor-Right Beef and Macaroni

2	cps (8 oz. pkg.) uncooked macaroni
2	tablespoons fat
1	clove garlic, split (insert wooden picks for easy removal)
½	cup (about 1 medium-size) chopped onion
¼	cup chopped green pepper
½	lb. ground beef
2½	cups (two 10½- or 11-oz. cans) condensed tomato soup
½	cup (4-oz. can) mushrooms
1	tablespoon Worcestershire sauce
1	teaspoon salt
½	teaspoon dry mustard
¼	teaspoon chili powder
4	oz. Swiss cheese
4	small (about 1 lb.) tomatoes
2	tablespoons butter or margarine melted

1. Grease a 2-qt. casserole and set out a large, heavy skillet having a tight-fitting cover.
2. Prepare macaroni.
3. Meanwhile, heat fat in the skillet.
4. Add garlic, onion and pepper and cook over medium heat about 5 min., stirring occasionally.
5. Add beef and cook until browned, breaking into small pieces with fork or spoon.
6. Add tomato soup, mushrooms, Worcestershire sauce, and a mixture of salt, dry mustard and chili powder slowly and blend well.
7. Stir until well blended. Cover; simmer 5 min.
8. Meanwhile, cut cheese into ¼-in. slices.
9. Rinse tomatoes, cut off stem ends and cut into ½-in. slices.
10. Remove garlic from meat mixture. Place one-half of the drained macaroni in casserole. Cover with one-half of the sauce. Repeat layering. Alternate cheese and tomato slices in a border around top of casserole.
11. Lightly brush tomato and cheese slices with melted butter or margarine.
12. Bake at 350°F 20 to 25 min., or until cheese is melted and lightly browned.

6 to 8 servings

Ham-Stuffed Eggplant

1	large (about 1½ lbs.) eggplant
1½	cups boiling water
¼	cup finely chopped onion
¼	cup finely chopped green pepper
2	cups ground cooked ham
1	cup fine cracker crumbs
1	cup (8-oz. can) tomato sauce
¼	cup (1 oz.) grated cheese
2	tablespoons melted butter

1. Set out a large, shallow baking dish and a 2-qt. saucepan having a tight-fitting cover.
2. Wash eggplant and cut into halves lengthwise.
3. Scoop out pulp with spoon, leaving shells ¼ to ½ in. thick. Place shells in baking dish, cut-sides up, and set aside.
4. Cut pulp into small pieces and put in the saucepan with ½ cup boiling water, onion and green pepper.
5. Cover and cook about 15 min., or until eggplant is tender.
6. Meanwhile, grind ham and set aside.
7. Prepare cracker crumbs and set aside.
8. Drain eggplant; add meat, one-half of cracker crumbs and tomato sauce.
9. Mix together lightly. Spoon mixture into eggplant shells.
10. Blend remaining cracker crumbs with grated cheese and melted butter.
11. Spoon mixture over tops of stuffed eggplant halves. Pour 1 cup boiling water around the eggplant in the baking dish.
12. Bake at 350°F 15 to 20 min., or until crumbs are golden brown.
13. Serve immediately.

4 to 6 servings

Veal-Mushroom Timbales

1	whole, canned pimiento
½	lb. mushrooms
3	tablespoons butter or margarine
2	tablespoons minced onion
2	cups ground cooked veal
1½	cups milk
⅓	cup fine, dry bread crumbs
2	tablespoons butter or margarine
1	teaspoon salt
⅛	teaspoon paprika
3	eggs, well beaten
	Tomato-Cheese Sauce (page 19)

1. Set out 8-in. skillet and a double boiler. Grease or oil (with salad or cooking oil—not olive oil) 8 heat resistant custard cups. Heat water for hot water bath.
2. Cut whole pimiento into thin crosswise strips.
3. Arrange 2 or 3 pimiento strips in bottom of each custard cup. Set aside.
4. Clean and slice mushrooms.
5. Heat in skillet butter or margarine.
6. Add mushrooms and minced onion to skillet.
7. Cook over medium heat, occasionally moving and turning with a spoon or fork until mushrooms are lightly browned. Set aside.
8. Grind cooked veal.
9. Combine in top of the double boiler milk, bread crumbs.
10. Place over simmering water until milk is scalded. Remove from simmering water. Blend in veal, onion, mushrooms, butter or margarine and a mixture of salt, and paprika.
11. Add gradually, vigorously blending mixture into eggs.
12. Fill custard cups two-thirds full with mixture. Set in the hot water bath.
13. Bake at 350 F 20 to 30 min., or until silver knife comes out clean when inserted in center of timbale. Run a spatula around inside of cups to loosen timbales. Unmold onto hot serving plates.
14. While timbales bake prepare Tomato-Cheese Sauce.
15. Serve sauce over unmolded timbales.

4 servings

Spinach-Veal Timbales: Follow recipe for Veal-Mushroom Timbales. Substitute 1 cup cooked **spinach,** well drained and finely chopped, for mushrooms and onion. Omit browning in butter or margarine.

Baked Luncheon Meat Favorites

1	12-oz. can luncheon meat (1½ to 2 cups, ground)
½	cup soft bread crumbs
¼	cup (about 1 oz.) finely chopped nuts
1	egg, beaten
2	teaspoons brown sugar
1	teaspoon dry mustard
¼	teaspoon paprika
1	8¼-oz. can sliced pineapple (about 4 slices pineapple)
2	tablespoons lemon juice
2	tablespoons brown sugar

1. Set out an 8x8x2-in. baking dish.
2. Grind contents of luncheon meat.
3. Combine soft bread crumbs, chopped nuts, and egg with meat and mix lightly.
4. Add a mixture of brown sugar, dry mustard and paprika. Set aside.
5. Drain can sliced pineapple, reserving ⅓ cup syrup.
6. Lay slices flat in bottom of baking dish.
7. Shape meat mixture into 4 patties the same size as pineapple slice. Put a patty on each pineapple slice.
8. Mix reserved pineapple syrup with lemon juice and brown sugar.
9. Spoon syrup mixture over patties.
10. Bake at 350°F 35 to 45 min. Baste patties with syrup mixture three or four times during cooking period.

4 servings

Lima Bean Casserole

1	**10-oz. pkg. frozen lima beans**
2½	**cups (3½ slices) soft bread crumbs**
¼	**cup milk**
1	**lb. ground beef**
1	**egg, beaten**
1	**small clove garlic, finely chopped**
1	**teaspoon salt**
¼	**teaspoon pepper**
1	**tablespoon fat**
¼	**cup water**
1½	**teaspoon salt**
½	**teaspoon pepper**
3	**tablespoons butter or margarine**
1	**cup thick sour cream**

1. Set out a large, heavy skillet and grease a 1½-qt. casserole.
2. Cook frozen lima beans.
3. Combine in a large bowl bread crumbs and milk.
4. Add ground beef, egg, and garlic.
5. Blend in a mixture of salt, and pepper.
6. Shape into balls about 1 in. in diameter.
7. Heat fat in the skillet. Add meat balls and brown over medium heat, turning occasionally to brown on all sides. Pour off fat as it collects. Remove meat balls from skillet and put in casserole. Pour water over meat balls.
8. Drain lima beans and season with a mixture of salt and pepper.
9. Add butter or margarine and mix thoroughly.
10. Cover meat balls with beans.
11. Bake, uncovered, at 350°F about 30 min. Remove from oven and spread with thick sour cream.
12. Return to oven and bake uncovered 5 min. longer.
13. Serve immediately.

About 4 servings

Scalloped Onions with Ham

2	**tablespoons butter or margarine**
⅓	**cup (1 slice) fine, dry bread crumbs**
1	**cup ground cooked ham**
6	**medium-size (about 1¼ lbs.) onions**
2	**cups Medium White Sauce (double recipe, page 17; add ½ teaspoon dry mustard to flour)**

1. Grease a 1½-qt. casserole and set out a small skillet.
2. Heat butter or margarine in the small skillet.
3. Stir in bread crumbs and set aside.
4. Grind cooked ham and set aside.
5. Clean onions and cook.
6. Meanwhile, prepare Medium White Sauce.
7. Blend the ground ham into the white sauce. Cover and set aside.
8. Drain the cooked onions and arrange in bottom of the casserole. Pour white sauce over onions. Sprinkle with buttered bread crumbs.
9. Bake at 400°F about 15 min., or until sauce is bubbling hot.

6 servings

Tamale Perfection

¼ lb. bulk pork sausage
1 cup (about 2 medium-size) finely chopped onion
½ cup finely chopped celery
⅓ cup finely chopped green pepper
1 lb. ground beef
2¼ cups canned tomatoes, sieved
1¼ cups (12-oz. can, drained) whole kernel corn
1 tablespoon salt
2 teaspoons chili powder
¼ teaspoon pepper
1 cup sliced ripe olives (about 16 large olives)
1 cup cold water
½ cup yellow corn meal
3 oz. sharp Cheddar cheese (¾ cup, grated)
6 whole ripe olives

1. Grease an 11x7x1½-in. baking dish.
2. Put pork sausage into a large, heavy, cold skillet having a tight-fitting cover.
3. Cook over medium heat. Break into small pieces with fork or spoon, pouring off fat as it collects.
4. Meanwhile, chop onion, celery and green pepper and set aside.
5. Add ground beef to skillet. Break into small pieces with a fork or spoon. Brown meat over medium heat, stirring occasionally. Pour off fat as it collects.
6. When meat begins to brown, add chopped onion, celery and green pepper. Cook until meat is well browned.
7. Gradually add canned tomatoes, whole kernel corn and a mixture of salt, chili powder, and pepper.
8. Cover and bring mixture to boiling over high heat. Reduce heat and simmer about 15 min.
9. Meanwhile, slice enough pitted ripe olives. Set aside.
10. Mix cold water and yellow corn meal together thoroughly.
11. Bring mixture in skillet to boiling; gradually add corn meal mixture while stirring constantly. Cook over medium heat, stirring slowly, until mixture is thickened. Mix in the sliced olives. Turn mixture into casserole.
12. Bake at 350°F about 1 hr.
13. Meanwhile, grate Cheddar cheese and set aside.
14. When mixture has baked 1 hr., remove casserole from oven and sprinkle the grated cheese over top of mixture. Return casserole to oven and bake about 5 min. longer, or until cheese is bubbly.
15. Garnish with whole ripe olives.
16. Cut into 6 servings. Serve immediately.

6 servings

Taco Casserole

1 pound ground beef
1 package (1.25 ounces) taco seasoning mix
1 cup water
1 can (15 ounces) refried beans with sausage
2 cups shredded lettuce
¼ cup chopped onion
1 tablespoon chopped green chilies
1 cup (4 ounces) shredded Cheddar cheese
Nacho-flavored tortilla chips
Chopped tomato
Sliced ripe olives
Dairy sour cream
Taco sauce

1. Brown ground beef in a skillet; drain off excess fat. Add taco mix and water. Simmer, uncovered, until mixture is thickened (about 15 minutes).
2. Lightly grease bottom of an 11 x 7-inch baking dish. Spread refried beans evenly on the bottom. Sprinkle with shredded lettuce, onion, and chilies; top with ground beef mixture. (If desired, cover and refrigerate until ready to finish.)
3. Bake, uncovered, at 400°F. 15 minutes. Sprinkle with shredded cheese and bake an additional 5 minutes, or until cheese is melted and mixture is heated through.
4. Remove from oven and garnish with tortilla chips.
5. Serve with chopped tomato, sliced olives, sour cream, and taco sauce in separate serving dishes.

6 servings

Shortcakes, Pinwheels and Pies

Ranch Shortcake

2	**Hard-Cooked Eggs** **Baking Powder Biscuits** **(page 16; roll dough to** **¹⁄₃-in. thickness and use a** **2¹⁄₂-in. cutter)**
2	**tablespoons fat**
1	**medium-size onion, thinly** **sliced**
1	**lb. ground beef**
2	**cups (two 8-oz. cans)** **tomato sauce**
1	**teaspoon Worcestershire** **sauce**
1	**teaspoon salt**
¹⁄₈	**teaspoon pepper**
1	**10-oz. pkg. frozen peas**

1. Set out a baking sheet and a large, heavy skillet having a cover.
2. Prepare eggs. Chop and set aside.
3. Prepare Baking Powder Biscuits and bake.
4. Meanwhile, heat fat in the skillet.
5. Add onion and cook, stirring occasionally, until tender.
6. Remove onion with slotted spoon and set aside.
7. Add beef to skillet, breaking into small pieces with fork or spoon.
8. Cook over medium heat until browned. Mix in the onion and add slowly, stirring in tomato sauce, Worcestershire sauce, and a mixture of salt and pepper.
9. Cover and simmer about 5 min.
10. Cook and drain contents of package frozen peas.
11. Add cooked peas and chopped eggs to skillet. Cook 3 to 5 min. longer, or until heated thoroughly.
12. Cut or tear biscuits into halves. Spoon sauce over half of biscuits and top with remaining halves.

4 to 6 servings

Cheese Ranch Shortcake: Follow recipe for Ranch Shortcake. *For Baking Powder Biscuits*—Grate 3 oz. **Cheddar cheese** (about ¾ cup, grated). Cut cheese into dry ingredients for biscuits with **lard.**

Upside-Down Ranch Shortcake: Follow recipe for Ranch Shortcake. Set temperature control of oven at 450°F. Prepare meat and vegetable sauce first; cover and simmer while preparing Baking Powder Biscuit dough. Roll dough into a round to fit top of skillet. Bring mixture to boiling and place dough on top of meat mixture in skillet. Put skillet in oven and bake 10 to 15 min., or until biscuit topping is golden brown. Cover with warm serving plate. Invert and remove skillet.

Veal Pot Pie

Baking Powder Biscuit dough (one-half recipe, page 16; add 1 teaspoon celery salt and 1½ teaspoons paprika to dry ingredients)

2   **medium-size carrots**
½   **cup (about 1 medium-size) chopped onion**
¼   **cup chopped green pepper**
2   **tablespoons fat**
¾   **lb. ground veal**
1¼   **cups (10½- to 11-oz. can) condensed cream of mushroom soup**
½   **cup milk**
2   **tablespoons minced parsley**
½   **teaspoon salt**
¼   **teaspoon pepper**

1. Set out a 1½-qt. casserole and a large, heavy skillet.
2. Prepare Baking Powder Biscuit dough .
3. Roll dough into a round ½ in. thick on a lightly floured surface. Using an even pressure to keep sides of biscuits straight, cut into rounds with a floured 2-in. cutter. Set aside.
4. Wash carrots, pare, thinly slice and set aside.
5. Prepare onion and pepper and set aside.
6. Heat fat in the skillet.
7. Add veal and cook over medium heat, breaking into small pieces with a fork or spoon.
8. When meat begins to brown, add vegetables and cook until carrots are tender, frequently moving and turning with fork or spoon. When carrots are tender, blend in mushroom soup, milk, parsley and a mixture of salt and pepper.
9. Simmer about 5 min. Bring just to boiling; turn into casserole. Arrange biscuits over top.
10. Bake at 450°F 10 to 15 min., or until biscuits are lightly browned.

About 6 servings

Cheese-Meat Pies

Pastry for Little Pies and Tarts (one-half recipe; page 15)

1   **tablespoon fat**
¼   **cup finely chopped onion**
½   **lb. ground beef**
¼   **lb. bulk pork sausage**
½   **cup (about 2 stalks) finely diced celery**
¼   **cup chopped green pepper**
¾   **teaspoon salt**
⅛   **teaspoon basil**
     Few grains cayenne pepper
¾   **cup tomatoes, sieved**
1½   **teaspoons Worcestershire sauce**
½   **lb. process cheese food**

1. Set out a large skillet.
2. Prepare Pastry for Little Pies and Tarts and bake in six 3½-in. tart pans.
3. Set aside.
4. Meanwhile, heat fat in the skillet.
5. Add onion and cook about 3 min.
6. Add beef and pork and cook over medium heat, breaking into small pieces with fork or spoon.
7. Pour off fat as it collects. When meat begins to brown, add celery, pepper, and a mixture of salt, basil and pepper and cook until celery and green pepper are tender.
8. Remove from heat and blend in tomatoes and Worcestershire sauce.
9. Simmer, uncovered, about 10 min., occasionally moving and turning mixture with a fork or spoon.
10. Meanwhile, set out cheese.
11. Grate about one-fourth of cheese food (about ½ cup, grated). Cut remaining cheese into six slices. Put one cheese slice in bottom of each baked pie shell. Fill with meat mixture. Sprinkle with the grated cheese.
12. Bake at 350°F 15 to 20 min.

6 servings

Taco Casserole 63

Ham Pinwheel Ring

1½   **cups ground cooked ham**
⅓   **cup sweetened condensed milk**
¼   **cup pickle relish**
2   **tablespoons minced parsley**
2   **teaspoons prepared mustard**
     Baking Powder Biscuit dough (page 16)
2   **tablespoons melted butter or margarine**
     Sauce Par Excellence (one-half recipe, page 20)

1. Set out a baking sheet.
2. Grind enough cooked ham to yield 1½ cups.
3. Combine milk, pickle relish, parsley, and prepared mustard with ham and mix lightly.
4. Set aside.
5. Prepare Baking Powder Biscuit dough.
6. Roll dough into a rectangle about ¼ in. thick on a lightly floured surface. Spread ham mixture evenly over biscuit dough. Starting with long side of dough, roll up and pinch long edge to seal. (Do not pinch ends of roll.) Place roll on baking sheet, sealed-edge down. Bring ends of roll together to form a ring. Brush ring lightly with melted butter or margarine.
7. With scissors or sharp knife, make cuts at 1 in. intervals around outside of ring to within ¼ in. of center. Slightly pull out and twist each section so that cut sides rest almost flat on baking sheet.
8. Bake at 400°F 20 to 30 min., or until ring is golden brown.
9. Meanwhile, prepare Sauce Par Excellence.
10. Serve ring with Sauce Par Excellence. Garnish with parsley.

6 to 8 servings

Beef Pinwheel Ring: Follow recipe for Ham Pinwheel Ring. Substitute 1½ cups ground cooked **beef** for ham. Add 1 teaspoon **salt** and ⅛ teaspoon **pepper** to meat mixture. Substitute **Tomato-Cheese Sauce** (one-half recipe, page 19) for Sauce Par Excellence.

Luncheon Meat Pinwheel Ring: Follow recipe for Ham Pinwheel Ring. Substitute 1½ cups ground **luncheon meat** for ham.

Teaser Ham Rolls

1   **cup ground cooked ham**
1   **medium-size banana with all-yellow or green-tipped peel (about ½ cup, mashed)**
2   **teaspoons minced onion**
½   **teaspoon prepared mustard**
     Few grains cayenne pepper
     Baking Powder Biscuit dough (page 16)
     Melted butter or margarine
1   **cup Mushroom-Cheese Sauce (one-half recipe, page 19)**

1. Set out a baking sheet.
2. Grind enough cooked ham to yield 1 cup.
3. Peel and mash banana.
4. Combine with ham and mix lightly, the mashed banana and onion, mustard and pepper.
5. Set aside.
6. Prepare Baking Powder Biscuit dough.
7. Roll dough into a square about ¼ in. thick. Cut into 3-in. squares. Spread about 2 tablespoons ham mixture evenly over each square. Roll up each square, pinching long edge to seal (do not pinch ends of roll). Put rolls on baking sheet, sealed edges down; brush with melted butter or margarine.
8. Bake at 400°F 20 to 30 min., or until rolls are lightly browned.
9. Meanwhile, prepare Mushroom-Cheese Sauce and set aside.
10. Serve ham rolls topped with Cheese-Mushroom Sauce.

About 4 servings

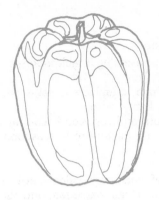

Ham Crescents: Follow recipe for Teaser Ham Rolls. Omit Mushroom-Cheese Sauce. Divide biscuit dough into halves. Roll each half into a round about ¼ in. thick. Spread each round with one-half of the ham mixture and cut each into 8 wedges. Roll each wedge, beginning at wide end. Put rolls on baking sheet with pointed edges down. Curve slightly to form crescents. Bake as in recipe.

Deep-Fried Pies

Pastry for Little Pies and Tarts (page 15)
⅓ cup finely chopped green pepper
¼ cup finely chopped carrot
¼ cup finely chopped celery
¼ cup (about 1 small) finely chopped onion
¼ cup (about 1 small) finely chopped green onion
1 tablespoon (about 1 medium) chopped hot red pepper
1 tablespoon chopped parsley
1 tablespoon chopped raisins
1 tablespoon chopped green olives
1 tablespoon capers
1 medium-size ripe tomato
¾ lb. ground beef
1 teaspoon salt
¼ teaspoon pepper
⅛ teaspoon cayenne pepper
2 tablespoons shortening
1½ teaspoons olive oil
¼ cup water
3 drops Tabasco
Hydrogenated vegetable shortening, all-purpose shortening, lard or cooking oil for deep-frying

1. Prepare Pastry for Little Pies and Tarts.
2. Shape into a ball, wrap in waxed paper, and place in refrigerator while preparing filling.
3. *For Meat Filling*—Set out a large skillet having a tight-fitting cover.
4. Prepare green pepper, carrot, celery, onion and green onion.
5. Add red pepper, parsley, raisins, green olives and capers.
6. Rinse and plunge tomato into boiling water to loosen skin.
7. Plunge tomato into cold water. Carefully remove and discard skin and stem end. Cut tomato into small pieces and add to chopped vegetable mixture.
8. Mix beef and a mixture of salt, pepper, and cayenne pepper lightly together.
9. Heat 2 tablespoons shortening and olive oil in the skillet over medium heat.
10. Add meat and cook until browned, breaking into small pieces with a fork or spoon. Add vegetable mixture and blend well. Blend water and Tabasco into hot mixture.
11. Cover and cook over low heat 30 min.
12. About 20 min. before deep-frying, fill a deep saucepan one-half to two-thirds full with hydrogenated vegetable shortening, all-purpose shortening, lard or cooking oil for deep-frying.
13. Heat slowly to 375°F.
14. Remove pastry from refrigerator and shape into two balls. Roll pastry to about ⅛-in. thickness (as in Pastry for Little Pies and Tarts). Using a lightly floured cookie cutter or a knife, cut into rounds about 4 in. in diameter. Place about 2 tablespoons filling onto each round. Moisten edges with cold water, fold pastry over, and press edges together. Flute or press edges with a fork. Be certain seal is tight.
15. Deep-fry only as many pies at one time as will lie flat and un-crowded one layer deep in fat. Deep-fry about 3 min., or until golden brown.
16. Turn pies as they rise to surface and several times during cooking (do not pierce). Drain over fat for a few seconds before removing to absorbent paper.

About 16 pies

Beef Roly Poly

4	slices Panbroiled Bacon (page 13)
1	12-oz. vacuum can whole kernel corn (about 1½ cups, drained)
1½	cups (2½ slices) soft bread crumbs
2	tablespoons minced onion
3	tablespoons water
½	teaspoon salt
¼	teaspoon marjoram
1/8	teaspoon pepper
½	lb. ground beef
½	lb. ground veal
¼	lb. ground pork
2	tablespoons minced celery leaves
1	egg, beaten
2	tablespoons water
1	teaspoon salt
¼	teaspoon garlic salt
1/8	teaspoon pepper

1. Grease a 9x9x2-in. baking dish.
2. *For Stuffing*—Prepare bacon, reserving 3 tablespoons bacon fat.
3. Put on absorbent paper to drain; crumble and set aside.
4. Drain contents of can whole kernel corn.
5. Using a fork, toss bacon, corn and reserved bacon fat with bread crumbs, onion, water, and a mixture of ½ teaspoon salt and ⅛ teaspoonpepper.
6. Set aside.
7. *For Meat Roll*—Combine beef, veal, pork, celery leaves, egg, water, and a mixture of 1 teaspoon salt, garlic salt, and ⅛ teaspoon pepper and mix together lightly.
8. Turn meat mixture onto a large sheet of waxed paper. Pat into a rectangle ½ in. thick. Spoon stuffing over meat and pat into an even layer, covering meat. Lift waxed paper along one long side of meat rectangle. Using paper as a guide, gently push meat into a firm roll. Lift waxed paper and roll carefully to baking dish; slide roll off paper into baking dish, open edge of roll on bottom to prevent unrolling during baking.
9. Bake at 350°F about 1 hr. With large spatulas or spoons, lift roll onto warm platter.

6 to 8 servings

Beef and Cheese Pie

	Pastry for 1-Crust Pie (page 15)
2	tablespoons fat
¾	lb. ground beef
1	cup (8-oz. can) tomato sauce
½	teaspoon Worcestershire sauce
¼	teaspoon salt
2	drops Tabasco
1	pkg. (3 oz.) cream cheese
½	cup (4 oz.) dry cottage cheese
¼	cup thick sour cream
2	tablespoons minced onion
1	tablespoon chopped green pepper
1	tablespoon chopped drained pimiento
¼	teaspoon salt

1. Set out a large, heavy skillet.
2. Prepare Pastry (but do not bake) for 1-Crust Pie in 8-in. pie pan.
3. Set aside.
4. Heat fat in the skillet.
5. Add beef and cook over medium heat until lightly browned, breaking into small pieces with fork or spoon.
6. Remove from heat and slowly blend in tomato sauce, Worcestershire sauce, ¼ teaspoon salt and Tabasco.
7. Simmer for 5 min. Set aside.
8. Put cream cheese in a small bowl and beat with fork until softened.
9. Blend one-half of the softened cream cheese with cottage cheese, sour cream, onion, green pepper, pimiento and ¼ teaspoon salt.
10. Carefully spread remaining softened cream cheese over pastry in pie pan. Turn cottage cheese mixture into pie pan over cream cheese layer and spread to edges. Cover with meat mixture.
11. Bake at 425°F 10 min.; reduce heat to 325°F and bake 30 min.

About 6 servings

Meat-Crusted Corn Pie

2	tablespoons butter or margarine
½	cup (about 1 medium-size) chopped onion
1	16-oz. can whole kernel corn (about 1¾ cups, drained)
1¼	cups (10½- to 11-oz. can) condensed tomato soup
1	teaspoon salt
½	teaspoon marjoram
¼	teaspoon chili powder
¾	lb. ground beef
¼	lb. ground pork
½	cup uncooked brown granular wheat cereal
1	egg, beaten
½	cup milk
3	tablespoons minced onion
1	tablespoons Worcestershire sauce
1	teaspoon salt
⅛	teaspoon pepper

1. Set out a 9-in. pie pan.
2. Heat butter or margarine in a large skillet.
3. Add onion and cook about 3 min.
4. Drain contents of can whole kernel corn.
5. Add tomato soup and a mixture of 1 teaspoon salt, marjoram and chili powder to the skillet, blending with fork or spoon.
6. Simmer, uncovered, about 10 min.
7. Meanwhile, mix beef, pork, wheat cereal, egg, milk, minced onion, Worcestershire sauce, and a mixture of 1 teaspoon salt and pepper lightly together.
8. Turn into pie pan. Gently pat mixture to evenly cover bottom, sides and rim of pan. Pour corn mixture into shell.
9. Bake at 350°F 35 to 40 min.
10. Garnish with green pepper rings.

About 6 servings

Meat-Crusted Lima Bean Pie: Follow recipe for Meat-Crusted Corn Pie. Substitute for corn, contents of 16-oz. can **lima beans,** drained (about 1½ cups).

Corn Bread-Crowned Meat and Bean Pie

1	12-oz. can luncheon meat (about 1½ cups, ground)
1	tablespoon fat
4	cups (two 16-oz. cans) baked beans in tomato sauce
½	cup (about 1 medium-size) chopped onion
½	cup tomato juice
¼	cup molasses
¼	cup ketchup
1	teaspoon dry mustard
½	cup sifted all-purpose flour
2	teaspoons sugar
1½	teaspoons baking powder
¼	teaspoon salt
½	cup yellow corn meal
1	egg, well beaten
½	cup milk
1	tablespoon shortening, melted

1. Grease a 2-qt. casserole. Set out a large skillet.
2. Grind contents of can luncheon meat.
3. Heat fat in the skillet.
4. Add ground luncheon meat and cook over medium heat, gently moving and turning occasionally, until lightly browned. Add to meat baked beans in tomato sauce, onion, tomato juice, molasses, ketchup and dry mustard, and mix thoroughly.
5. Simmer 8 to 10 min.
6. *For Corn Bread Topping*—Sift together flour, sugar, baking powder and salt into a bowl.
7. Mix in corn meal.
8. Blend egg, milk and shortening thoroughly.
9. Make a well in center of dry ingredients and add liquid mixture all at one time. Stir vigorously only until dry ingredients are moistened, being careful not to overmix. Bring bean mixture to boiling. Turn into casserole. Immediately drop corn bread batter by spoonfuls evenly over top. (Corn bread will spread together during baking to form a topping.
10. Bake at 400°F 20 to 25 min., or until a wooden pick or cake tester comes out clean when inserted gently in center of corn bread.

6 to 8 servings

Pork Brown Sauce on Sweet Potato Biscuits

1	medium-size sweet potato
1¼	cups sifted all-purpose flour
1	tablespoon baking powder
1	tablespoon sugar
1	teaspoon salt
½	cup lard, hydrogenated vegetable shortening or all-purpose shortening
½	cup milk or cream
2	cups Quick Meat Broth (double recipe, page 10)
1	tablespoon molasses
2	teaspoons soy sauce
½	teaspoon salt
¼	teaspoon paprika
⅛	teaspoon pepper
¾	cup (1 to 2 medium-size) washed, pared or scraped and sliced carrots
½	cup (about 1 medium-size) chopped onion
¼	cup finely chopped green pepper
1	teaspoon fat
1	lb. ground pork
1	3¼-oz. can sliced mushrooms (about ⅓ cup, drained)
½	cup water
¼	cup all-purpose flour

1. *For Sweet Potato Biscuits*—Set out a baking sheet.
2. Wash potato, scrub with a vegetable brush and cook covered in boiling salted water to cover.
3. Cook 20 to 30 min., or until potato is tender when pierced with a fork.
4. Meanwhile, sift together flour, baking powder, sugar and 1 teaspoon salt.
5. Cut lard, hydrogenated vegetable shortening or all-purpose shortening into dry ingredients with a pastry blender or two knives until mixture resembles coarse corn meal.
6. When sweet potato is cooked, drain, peel and mash. Add ¾ cup of the mashed sweet potato to flour-lard mixture; blend in thoroughly. Make a well in center of mixture and add milk or cream all at one time.
7. Stir with a fork until just blended. Drop by large spoonfuls onto baking sheet, forming 8 large biscuits.
8. Bake at 400°F 20 to 30 min., or until lightly browned.
9. *For Pork Brown Sauce*—Set out a large, heavy skillet having a tight-fitting cover.
10. Prepare Quick Meat Broth.
11. Blend in molasses, soy sauce, and a mixture of ½ teaspoon salt, paprika and pepper, and set aside.
12. Prepare carrots, onion and green pepper and set aside.
13. Heat fat in the skillet.
14. Add pork and cook over medium heat, breaking into pieces with fork or spoon.
15. Pour off fat as it collects.
16. Meanwhile, drain contents of can sliced mushrooms.
17. As the pork begins to brown, add chopped vegetables and mushrooms. Cook until meat is well browned, occasionally moving and turning mixture with fork or spoon. Remove from heat and slowly pour in meat broth mixture. Cover and simmer about 15 min.
18. Meanwhile, put water into a 1-pt. screw-top jar.
19. Sprinkle flour evenly onto water.
20. Cover jar tightly and shake until well blended. Bring contents of skillet to boiling. Shake contents of jar again and slowly pour into skillet while moving and turning mixture with a fork or spoon. Bring mixture to boiling and cook 3 to 5 min. Cover and simmer about 10 min. longer.
21. Split sweet potato biscuits into halves; serve with meat sauce between halves.

4 to 6 servings

Pork Brown Sauce in Whipped Potato Ring: Follow recipe for Pork Brown Sauce on Sweet Potato Biscuits. Omit Sweet Potato Biscuits. Prepare **Whipped Potato Ring** (page 14). Pour Pork Brown Sauce into center of ring. Garnish with **parsley** and **carrot flowers**.

Grill It Outdoors

The Equipment—You will need a few accessories besides your grill—fuel, a skillet, a long-handled fork and a spoon, an asbestos mitt or heavy pot holder, and metal skewers. Paper napkins or towels—in quantity—are an essential part of outdoor cooking and service, for properly grilled foods are meant to be wonderfully juicy.

The Fire—Charcoal lumps or briquets and hard or fruit woods are the best fuel. Start with a good bed of charcoal, 2 to 3 inches deep. (It should last the entire cooking period.) Sprinkle a charcoal lighter fluid over the fuel and ignite. You'll find plenty to keep you busy while you wait for the coals to burn to a gray color with a ruddy glow underneath. This is your cooking fire which gives a hot, sustained, glowing heat. Allow 30 minutes for your fire to become a bed of coals ready for grilling.

Dampened hickory chips tossed on a charcoal fire just before the meat is placed on the grill create a hickory smoke with gives an added flavor touch.

Another way to start the fire is by beginning the bed with a small amount of paper and kindling. Add a small amount of charcoal and when it is burning, build the entire bed as directed.

Timing of cooking periods will vary with the size of the firebox, degree of heat, amount and direction of wind and type of grill used. Timings and distances given here are only guides. If dripping fat starts a flare-up, use a baster to douse the flames with sparing applications of water.

The Food—Ground meat adapts itself to the grill in several ways.

On the Grill—You may season it, shape it gently into patties, and turn out the universally esteemed hamburger or any of its relatives. With the addition of a few vegetables, grilled to perfection, a tasty bill-of-fare is created.

In the Skillet—Tender ground meat may be cooked over the grill in any of a variety of zestful sauces. Most of the recipes for burgers and balls prepared in a skillet are adaptable to the grill.

Now, combine all the mixin's and the world of grilling is yours for the trying.

Marinade

1   tablespoon sugar
1   teaspoon salt
1   teaspoon dry mustard
1   teaspoon paprika
¼   teaspoon celery salt
¾   cup salad oil or olive oil
¼   cup cider vinegar, tarragon
     vinegar or lemon juice
1   clove garlic

1. Mix sugar, salt, dry mustard, paprika and celery salt in a bowl or screw-top jar.
2. Add salad oil or olive oil and cider vinegar, tarragon vinegar or lemon juice.
3. Beat mixture with a rotary beater or shake until well blended. Add garlic.
4. Store, covered, in refrigerator. Before using, beat or shake thoroughly; remove garlic.

Grilled Hamburger Favorites

1   lb. ground beef
1   teaspoon salt
¼   teaspoon pepper
     Melted butter (or
     Marinade)

1. Put beef into a bowl.
2. Mix salt and pepper lightly into beef.
3. Shape into four patties. Put patties in greased steak broiler or directly onto greased grill at least 5-in. from top of coals. Grill about 4 min., or until browned on one side.
4. Turn patties and brush with melted butter (or Marinade).
5. Grill patties until second side is browned. Serve on toasted buns. Have one or more of the following on hand: chili sauce, prepared mustard, pickles, olives, onion slices, or tomato slices.
6. *To Toast Buns*—Cut buns into halves and brush cut sides with melted butter. Place on grill and toast cut side. Add more melted butter and serve the buns hot. For extra crispness, toast uncut side a moment before serving.

4 hamburgers

Note: Chopped **dill pickles, chives,** toasted **nuts,** chopped **mushrooms** or **sesame seed** blended into the meat mixture offer pleasing variations in flavor. Or, for extra zip blend in **ketchup, pickle relish, Worcestershire Sauce, chili powder** or **prepared horse-radish.**

Cheeseburgers: Follow recipe for Grilled Hamburger Favorites. When second side of patties is partially browned, place **Cheddar cheese slice** on each patty. (The cheese will melt slightly over the burger.)

Barbecued Burgers: Follow recipe for Grilled Hamburger Favorites. Substitute **Barbecue Sauce** (page 74) for butter. When first side is browned, turn and brush patty with Barbecue Sauce, using pastry brush.

Hawaiian Burgers: Follow recipe for Grilled Hamburger Favorites. Drain contents of 15¼-oz. can **pineapple slices.** Place slices on grill with hamburgers. Brush with **melted butter.** Brown pineapple slices 4 to 5 min. on each side. Top hamburgers with pineapple slices.

Surprise Hamburgers: Follow recipe for Grilled Hamburger Favorites. Shape twice as many patties by making them thinner. Place a **Cheddar cheese slice** on each of 4 patties. Top cheese slices with remaining patties. Press edges to seal. Wrap one slice of **bacon** around outside edge of each patty and fasten to patty with a wooden pick. Grill as in recipe.

Sandwich-Style Hamburgers: Follow recipe for Grilled Hamburger Favorites. Shape twice as many patties by making them thinner. Spread 4 patties with a mixture of 2 teaspoons **olive oil** and 8 teaspoons **Roquefort** or **Blue cheese.** Top with remaining patties and press edges together.

Grilled Lamb-Burgers: Follow recipe for Grilled Hamburger Favorites. Substitute ground **lamb** for ground beef. Add ¼ teaspoon **dill seed** or 2 tablespoons chopped **mint leaves** to the meat.

Dinner on a Grill

4   **ears garden-fresh corn**
4   **baking potatoes**
1   **tablespoon butter**
    Few grains salt
    Few grains paprika
4   **Spanish or Bermuda onions**
    Grilled Hamburger Favorites (page 72) or any variation (omit buns)
2   **large tomatoes**
    Melted butter
    Salt
    Pepper

1. *For Roast Corn*—Select corn with long stem ends for easier handling and turning.
2. Loosen husks only enough to remove silks and blemishes from corn.
3. Dip ears in a deep pail of water. Shake well. Rewrap husks around corn. Plunge in water again and let stand until husks are soaked (about 1 hr.). Place ears on grill or in steak broiler over hot coals allowing stem ends to extend beyond end of grill. Roast, turning often, until tender (about 15 min.).
4. Husk and serve with butter.
5. *F or Baked Potatoes*—Wash potatoes, scrub, wipe dry.
6. Rub fat over entire surface of potatoes and wrap each loosely in aluminum foil. Seal open ends with a double fold. Place on grill and bake about 1 hr., or until potatoes are soft when pressed with the fingers (protected by pot holder or asbestos gloves). Turn several times for even baking.
7. Cut cross in top of each potato and pinch open. Place butter, salt and paprika in center of each.
8. Skins and all are edible when potatoes are baked this way.
9. *For Grilled Onions*—Leave outside skins on onions.
10. Wet each onion thoroughly. Place on grill; roll onions occasionally while grilling. Onions are done when black on the outside and soft and creamy on the inside (about 50 min).
11. *For Hamburgers*—Prepared Grilled Hamburger Favorites or any variation (omit buns).
12. *For Grilled Tomatoes*—Cut tomatoes into halves crosswise.
13. Brush with butter.
14. Season with salt and pepper.
15. Place on grill, cut-side up, for about 3 min.

4 servings

Note: Grilled **marshmallows** are as much fun to grill for dessert as they are to eat.

Ground Meat in Barbecue Sauce

1   **cup ketchup**
½   **cup water**
2   **tablespoons sugar**
2   **tablespoons prepared mustard**
2   **tablespoons vinegar**
2   **teaspoons Worcestershire sauce**
2   **tablespoons butter**
1   **cup (2 medium size) chopped onion**
2   **lbs. ground beef**
2   **teaspoons salt**
½   **teaspoon pepper**

1. *For Barbecue Sauce*—Combine in a 1-pt. screw top jar, ketchup, water, sugar, prepared mustard, vinegar and Worcestershire sauce.

2. Cover and shake until blended.

3. *For Meat Mixture*—Heat butter in skillet on a grill.

4. Add onion and cook until onion is tender.

5. Add beef and a mixture of salt and pepper, breaking beef apart with spoon or fork.

6. When meat is browned, blend in sauce. Put skillet on back of grill and cook slowly about 15 min. Spoon meat and sauce into buttered buns.

4 to 6 servings

Note: Sauce may be prepared in advance and stored in refrigerator.

Mincemeat Specialties

Mincemeat

¼	lb. suet
1½	cups ground cooked beef
4	medium-size apples (about 3 cups, chopped)
1	cup firmly packed brown sugar
1	cup apple cider
½	cup fruit jelly
½	cup raisins, chopped
½	cup currants
2	tablespoons molasses
1	teaspoon salt
1	teaspoon cinnamon
½	teaspoon cloves
½	teaspoon nutmeg
¼	teaspoon mace
1	tablespoon grated lemon peel
1	tablespoon lemon juice

1. Set out a large, heavy skillet.
2. Grind suet and enough cooked beef to yield 1½ cups.
3. Set aside suet and beef.
4. Wash apples, quarter, core, pare and chop.
5. Put apples and meat in skillet, add brown sugar, apple cider, fruit jelly, raisins, currants, molasses, and a mixture of salt, cinnamon, cloves, nutmeg and mace, and mix thoroughly.
6. Stirring occasionally, simmer uncovered about 1 hr., or until most of liquid is absorbed. Add lemon peel and lemon juice.
7. Blend thoroughly.

3½ cups Mincemeat

Note: If mincemeat is not used immediately, pack hot mincemeat into sterilized jars and seal. Cool away from draft; label and store in a cool, dry place.

Lattice Mincemeat Pie

	Pastry for 1-Crust Pie (page 15)
1	large apple (about 1¼ cups, chopped)
3½	cups Mincemeat (on this page)
⅔	cup butter or margarine
¼	cup brandy
2	cups sifted confectioners' sugar
⅛	teaspoon salt

1. Prepare (but do not bake) Pastry for 1-Crust Pie in a 9-in. pie pan.
2. Set aside.
3. Wash apple, quarter, core, pare and chop.
4. Put apple in saucepan with Mincemeat.
5. Heat mixture thoroughly. Fill pastry shell with mincemeat mixture.
6. Bake at 400°F 30 to 35 min. Cool pie on cooling rack.
7. Meanwhile, prepare hard sauce.
8. *For Brandy Hard Sauce*—Cream butter or margarine until softened.
9. Add brandy gradually, beating in.
10. Add confectioners' sugar and salt gradually, creaming until fluffy after each addition.
11. When pie is cool, force hard sauce through a pastry bag and No. 27 star tube in long strips to form a crisscross design over top of pie.
12. Serve immediately.

One 9-in. pie

Mincemeat Cake Roll

1   **cup sifted cake flour**
¼   **teaspoon salt**
4   **egg yolks**
½   **cup sugar**
¼   **cup water**
1½   **teaspoons vanilla extract**
4   **egg whites**
½   **teaspoon cream of tartar**
½   **cup sugar**
    Sifted confectioners' sugar
1¾   **cups Mincemeat (½ recipe, page 75)**

1. Grease bottom of a 15½x10½x1-in. cake pan; line with waxed paper cut to fit bottom of pan; grease again.
2. Sift flour and salt together and set aside.
3. Beat egg yolks, sugar, water and vanilla extract until very thick and lemon colored.
4. Gently fold in dry ingredients until well blended. Set aside.
5. Beat egg whites until frothy.
6. Add cream of tartar and beat slightly.
7. Add sugar gradually, beating thoroughly after each addition.
8. Continue beating until very stiff peaks are formed. Gently spread egg yolk mixture over egg whites and carefully fold together until blended. Turn batter into pan and spread evenly to edges.
9. Bake at 350°F 20 to 25 min., or until a wooden pick or cake tester, inserted in center of cake comes out clean.
10. Immediately loosen edges of cake with a sharp knife; turn onto clean towel sprinkled with confectioners' sugar.
11. Carefully remove paper and cut off any crisp edges of cake. To roll, begin rolling nearest edge of cake. Using towel as a guide, tightly grasp nearest edge of towel and quickly pull it over beyond opposite edge. Cake will roll itself as you pull. Wrap cake in towel and set on cooling rack to cool (about ½ hr.).
12. Shortly before ready to serve, unroll cake and spread with Mincemeat.
13. Carefully reroll cake. Cut filled cake roll into crosswise pieces and serve.

1 cake roll

Spicy Filled Vienna Bread

1   **loaf Vienna or French bread**
2   **cups soft bread crumbs**
1   **lb. ground beef**
1   **cup Mincemeat (about one-fourth recipe, page 75)**
1   **cup (4 oz.) grated American cheese**
2   **tablespoons minced onion**
3   **tablespoons apple juice**
1   **egg, beaten**
1   **teaspoon salt**
¼   **teaspoon pepper**
    Melted butter or margarine

1. Set out a baking sheet.
2. Cut a thin lengthwise slice from top of French bread.
3. Set slice aside. With a small, sharp knife, cut down around edge of loaf, ¾ in. from edges, keeping shell intact. Pull out soft center and set loaf shell aside.
4. Using bread removed from center of loaf, prepare bread crumbs.
5. Combine crumbs with beef, Mincemeat , American cheese, onion, apple juice, egg and a mixture of salt and pepper.
6. Mix lightly. Pack lightly into bread shell. Set loaf on baking sheet.
7. Bake at 350°F about 1 hr. To lightly toast slice from top of bread, brush it generously with melted butter or margarine.
8. Set it on baking sheet 15 min. before end of baking period.
9. Fasten toasted bread slice to top of bread loaf with wooden picks. Slice and serve.

8 servings

Individual Beef Stuffed Loaves: Follow recipe for Spicy Filled Vienna Bread. Sutstitute 6 to 8 large **French rolls** for loaf of bread. Bake loaves at 350°F 30 to 45 min. Toast top slices during last 10 min. of baking period. Omit final slicing.

Mincemeat Bars

1¾	cups Mincemeat (one-half recipe, page 75)
1½	cups sifted all-purpose flour
1	teaspoon baking soda
½	teaspoon salt
½	teaspoon nutmeg
¼	teaspoon mace
1¾	cups uncooked rolled oats
½	cup shortening
¼	teaspoon lemon extract
1	cup firmly packed brown sugar
⅓	cup cream

1. Lightly grease an 11x7x1¼-in. pan.
2. Prepare Mincemeat and set aside.
3. Sift together flour, baking soda, salt, nutmeg and mace.
4. Mix in rolled oats and set aside.
5. Beat together shortening and lemon extract.
6. Add brown sugar gradually, creaming until fluffy after each addition.
7. Measure cream.
8. Mix in one half of dry ingredients; mix in cream. Finally add remaining dry ingredients, mixing until well blended. (Mixture will be crumbly.)
9. Divide dough into two portions. Firmly press one portion into pan. Spread mincemeat over dough in pan in an even layer. Top with remaining dough, patting until smooth.
10. Bake at 350°F about 30 min.
11. Remove pan to cooling rack. Cut into bars about 2¼x1-in.

About 3 doz. bars

Mincemeat Cupcakes

¼	cup butter or margarine
¾	cup firmly packed brown sugar
1¾	cups Mincemeat (one-half recipe, page 75)
½	cup (about 2 oz.) chopped nuts
2	cups sifted cake flour
1	tablespoon baking powder
¾	teaspoon salt
⅔	cup hydrogenated vegetable shortening, all-purpose shortening, butter or margarine
½	teaspoon orange extract
1	cup sugar
⅔	cup milk
4	egg whites

1. Generously butter 24 2½-in. muffin pan wells.
2. *For Topping*—Combine margarine and brown sugar in a saucepan.
3. Cook over low heat until well blended, stirring constantly. Remove the mixture from heat and blend in Mincemeat and chopped nuts.
4. Put 1 to 2 tablespoons of this mixture in each muffin pan well. Set aside.
5. *For Cake*—Sift together cake flour, baking powder and salt and set aside.
6. Beat together hydrogenated vegetable shortening, all-purpose shortening, butter or margarine and orange extract.
7. Add ½ cup sugar gradually, beating until fluffy after each addition.
8. Measure milk.
9. Alternately blend dry ingredients in fourths, milk in thirds, into creamed mixture, beating only until smooth after each addition. Finally beat only until batter is smooth (do not overbeat).
10. Beat egg whites until frothy.
11. Add ½ cup sugar gradually, beating well after each addition.
12. Continue beating the meringue until very stiff peaks are formed. Gently slide beaten egg whites over batter and fold together.
13. Spoon batter into muffin pan wells over mincemeat mixture. Fill each well one-half to two-thirds full.
14. Bake at 350°F about 20 min., or until cake tester or wooden pick inserted in center of cupcake comes out clean or until cakes spring back when lightly touched in center. Invert muffin pans onto cooling racks. Remove pans.
15. Serve cupcakes with unsweetened whipped cream.

2 doz. cupcakes

Index